SMART DOLPHIN ZONE

one 1

English for Elementary

by Patricia Avila

DATOS EDITORIALES

Published by UnilX Education
books@unilxeducation.com
USA +1 619 798 6274
MEX +52 6631030487

MyEnglishGameZone®, 2021 ©UnilX LLC, 2021

All rights reserved. No part of this publication may be reproduced, stored in a retrieval system, or transmitted in any form or by any means, electronic, mechanical, photocopying, recording, or otherwise, without the prior permission of the copyright owner.

First Published 2021

Author: Patricia Armida Ávila Delfín
Main Characters: My English Game Zone®
Cover and Complimentary Graphics: UnilX, Innovalingua Design Team and Freepik.com
Illustration, Design and Animation Leader: Rafael Orellana
Proofreader: Sandra Rojas
Editorial Design: UNIGRÁPHICA
    Rogelio Núñez Osuna
    José Chairez Parda
    Siham Núñez Osuna
    Julieta García García

PROGRAM SYNOPSIS

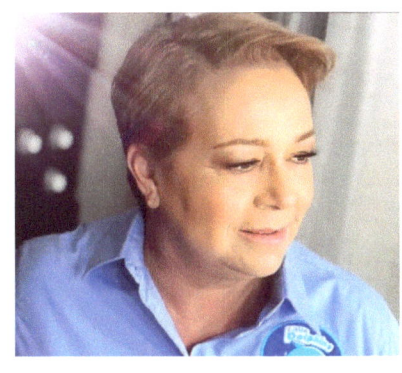

The fundamental objective of Smart Dolphin Zone is learning to communicate through interaction in the target language. The Theory of Language learning tells us that "language is a tool for communication and that students learn a language by using it to communicate."

You will find that Smart Dolphin Zone is a series based on guided everyday communicative interaction. E.g. when students are faced with real life dialogs to find out the schedule of the week's exams or to describe a classmate by his/her physical appearance, among many other authentic situations. Guided dialogs provide opportunities for language learners to interact with each other or with native speakers while feeling comfortable doing so.

This series also acknowledges the role of grammar as that of great importance for our learners to reach higher levels of proficiency and introduces the basic structures from the start of the program.

Smart Dolphin Zone also makes extensive use of authentic texts like: songs, jokes, rhymes, tongue twisters and popular children's stories. They will enrich the knowledge of culture through language.

As you can see, Smart Dolphin Zone has a solid base on the most important methodologies necessary to enhance the learning of the second language in a **dynamic** and **fun** way.

Patricia Avila Delfín

METHODOLOGIES

Vocabulary Learning

Vocabulary learning is central to language acquisition.

Specialists emphasize the need for a systematic and principled approach of vocabulary by the teacher and the learner. Teaching techniques and activities state that new words should not be learned by simple rote memorization.

It is important that new vocabulary items be presented in contexts rich enough to provide clues to meaning and that students be given multiple exposure to items they should learn.

Communicative Language Learning

Learning to communicate through interaction in the target language is the principal characteristic of the *Communicative Language Teaching* approach.

The *Theory of Language Learning* states that:
• Language is a tool for communication
• Students learn a language by using it to communicate

Integrated Skills Approach

The four basic skills in language teaching are: listening, speaking, reading, writing.

When we acquire a second language in a natural way the skills appear in that same order.

But why should we integrate the four skills when teaching the second language? If we are focused on teaching a realistic communication competence, the four skills must be developed in an integrated way.

Integrating the skills allows us to use more variety in the lessons because the range of activities will be ampler.

Spiral Learning

Learning should work like a game in a spiral, that gets a child interested while repeating and gradually increasing difficulty. It also gives students challenging activities and at the same time adds new skills.

The steps to achieve Spiral Learning are:
• Introduce new language. Move forward.
• Recap the important language learned so far.
• Add more language.
• Recap selected language: recent and earlier.
• Repeat the process.

Topic Based Approach

Topic based approach is student-centered. It helps with students' attention span.

It will hold students' interest from the start to the end of the lesson.

COURSE STRUCTURE

Book number	CEFR	LEVELS (12)	NUMBER OF UNITS (180)	NUMBER OF LESSONS (900)
1	Pre- A1	1	15	75
		2	15	75
2	A1.1	3	15	75
	A1.2	4	15	75
3	A2.1	5	15	75
		6	15	75
4	A2.2	7	15	75
		8	15	75
5	B1.1	9	15	75
	B1.2	10	15	75
6	B1.3	11	15	75
	B+	12	15	75

SERIES FEATURES

- Each book with 30 units.
- Two different levels in each book.
- Each unit has five lessons:

Lesson 1: Vocabulary
In this first lesson the vocabulary that will be used during the rest of the unit will be presented through clear images that represent each word.

Lesson 2: Dialogs
The dialogs will recap the vocabulary items from lesson one and use them in everyday real situations.

Lesson 3: Reading
The reading texts will go from original stories that take the ideas of the dialogs and complete them in a text to popular stories from children's literature.

Lesson 4: Writing
Prompted writing is used in the lower levels. It encourages students to use their imagination to come up with new and creative ideas for the text. In the higher levels, students will be asked to arrange the paragraphs or the missing sentences to complete the stories they read before.

Lesson 5: Language in Use
The last part of each unit, recaps the grammar structures seen, through the presentation of language in use of the four lessons before it. There are activities that will evaluate the knowledge acquired.

CONTENTS MAP

LEVEL CEFR	UNIT	TOPIC	VOCABULARY	LANGUAGE IN USE	CAN DO STATEMENT
1 PRE-A1	1	Let's play with the alphabet!	Characters, Alphabet	Song: ABC's song	I can identify the letters of the alphabet. I can give personal information.
	2	Let's play with numbers!	Numbers 1-10	Song: This is old man	I can say how old I am. I can recognize numbers.
	3	Let's play with classroom language!	Classroom language	Song: Mary had a little lamb	I can understand simple instructions given by the teacher during the class.
	4	Let's play with the weather!	Days of the week Weather	Verb BE = IS. Capital letters for days of the week.	I can understand days of the week. I can understand the words for different types of weather.
	5	Let's play at school!	Rooms at school	Demonstrative pronouns	I recognize words from my school.
	6	Let's play at school!	Classroom objects	Simple question BE Affirmative answers	I can understand familiar words and phrases about My school.
	7	Let's play with school objects!	School objects	Prepositions Personal pronouns	I can match words and sentences to pictures.
	8	Let's play with colors and shapes!	Colors Shapes	Adjectives (colors) Negative answers BE	I can recognize shapes and colors.
	9	Let's play with my family!	Family members	Possessive adjective MY Who	I can name the family members.
	10	Let's play at home!	Rooms at home	Short negative answer Where Colors to describe rooms	I can identify the names of the parts of the house.
	11	Let's play family at home!	More family members More rooms	Personal pronouns: he, she, it	I can identify familiar words and familiar objects.
	12	Let's play with emotions!	Emotions	Question words: Who, what, where, how	I can understand the words for feelings.
	13	Let's play with clothes!	Clothes	Demonstrative pronouns these - those	I can understand the words of clothes that I wear.
	14	Let's play at the store!	Clothes Adjectives Colors	There is- are Affirmative interrogative negative	I can understand the words of the clothes that I wear.
	15	Let's play with the prices!	Adjectives	How much? (for prices)	I can understand when someone says the price of an object.

CONTENTS MAP

LEVEL CEFR	UNIT	TOPIC	VOCABULARY	LANGUAGE IN USE	CAN DO STATEMENT
2 PRE-A1	16 / 1	Let's play at school!	Class activities	Present progressive; affirmative, interrogative, negative	I can understand the names of food that I eat.
	17 / 2	Let's play with food!	Food	Present progressive Wh questions	I can identify familiar words and phrases.
	18 / 3	Let's play at home!	Home activities	Present progressive Wh-doing?	I can identify familiar words and phrases about home.
	19 / 4	Let's play at home!	Home activities	Present progressive affirmative, negative, wh questions	I can identify familiar actions.
	20 / 5	Let's play at home!	Home activities rooms at home	Possessive adjectives	I can identify activities at home.
	21 / 6	Let's play on the move!	Transportation	Can affirmative	I can understand some words of traveling.
	22 / 7	Let's play with animals!	Animals	Can Negative	I can identify the names of animals.
	23 / 8	Let's play with the senses!	Body parts-senses	Can Interrogative	I can understand some words of the parts of my body.
	24 / 9	Let's play every day!	Verbs	Present simple affirmative	I can understand familiar words and phrases of habitual actions.
	25 / 10	Let's play community helpers!	Community helpers/ activities	Present simple 3rd person singular	I can identify familiar words and phrases.
	26 / 11	Let's play healthy habits!	Health habits	Present simple interrogative -DO	I can understand the names for people who work and live in my town.
	27 / 12	Let's play with animals!	Animals	Present simple Interrogative DOES	I can identify the names of places around the city.
	28 / 13	Let's play with animals!	Animals	Present simple Negative don't-doesn't	I can understand the names of some animals
	29 / 14	Let's play with the buildings in town!	Buildings community helpers activities	Present Simple Wh- questions	I can understand the names of some animals.
	30 / 15	Let's play with languages!	Languages nationalities	Countries nationalities languages	I recognize the names of countries in the world.

Level ONE Unit ONE
Let's play with the alphabet!

1.1 Dialogs

Practice the following dialogs

Good morning my name is Miss Patty.
What's your name?
-Hello! My name is Sandy

Hi! My name is Tony.
What's Your name?
-Good morning!
-My name is Lucy.

Hello! My name is Andy.
What's your name?
-Hello! My name is…
           (your name)

Ask your classmate's name.
Good morning!
My name is _____
WHAT'S YOUR NAME?

_____

Match the names to your new friends

Andy

Lucy

Sandy

Tony

Miss Paty

1.2 Vocabulary

Level ONE Unit ONE
Let's play with the alphabet!

Learn the alphabet

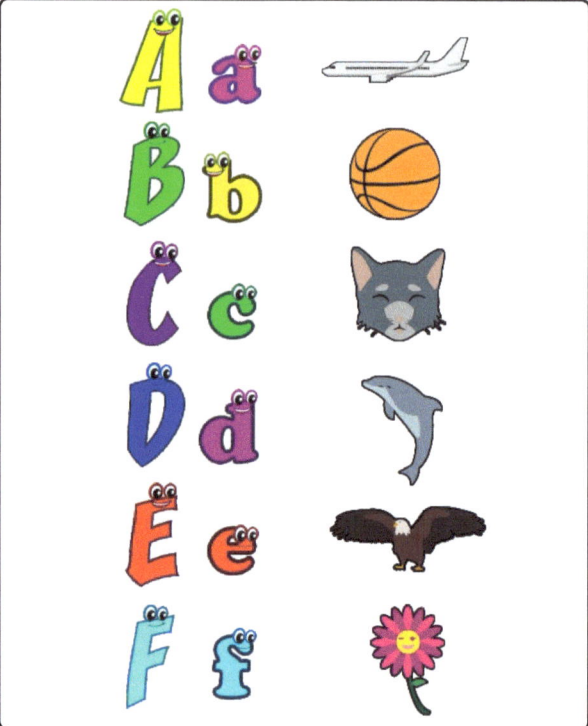

Level ONE Unit ONE
Let's play with the alphabet!

1.3 Reading

Match the letter with its picture

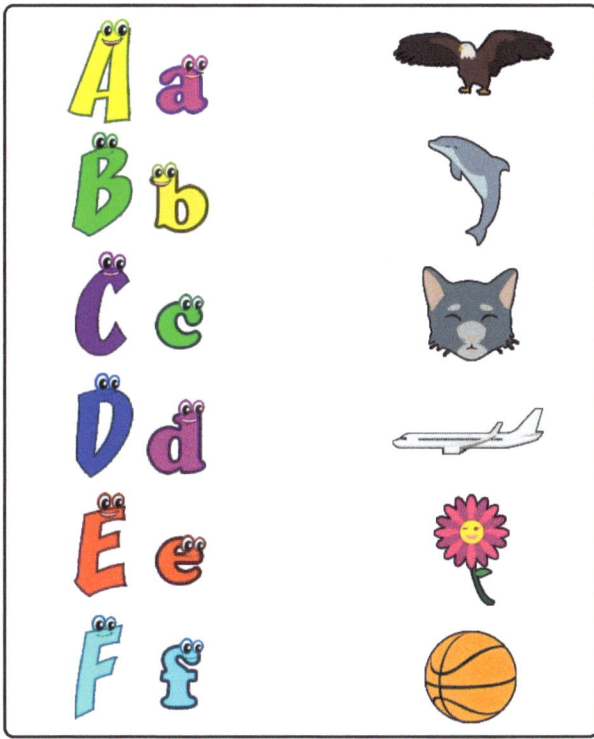

Level ONE Unit ONE
Let's play with the alphabet!

Trace each capital and small letter. Say it aloud.

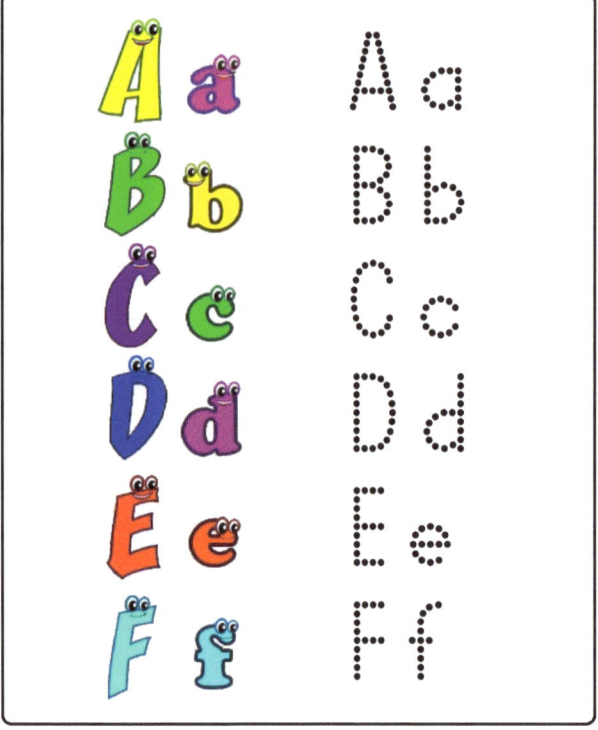
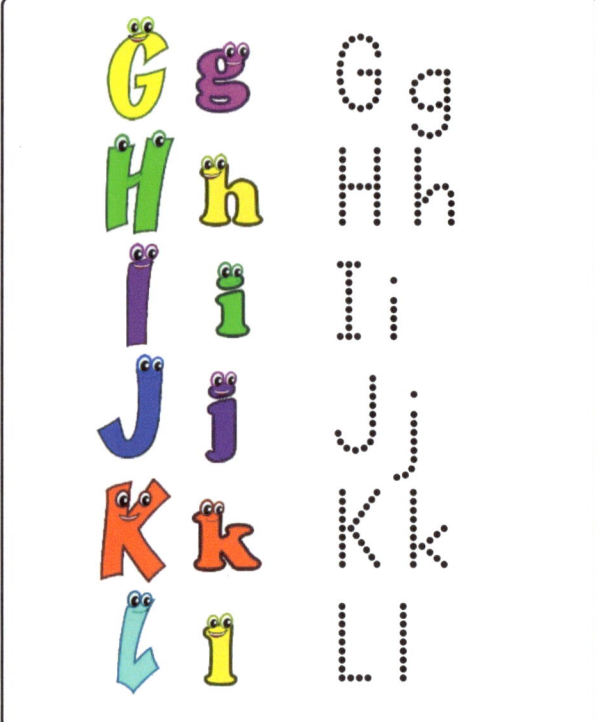
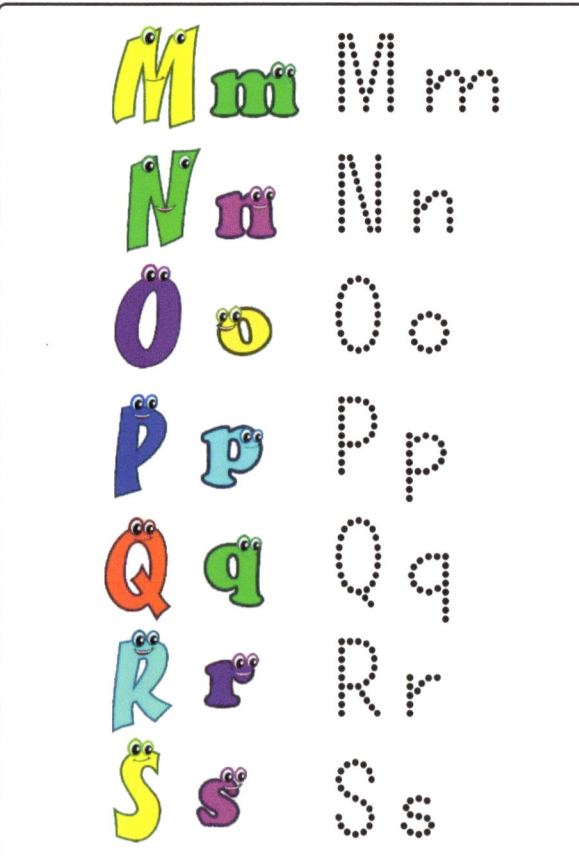
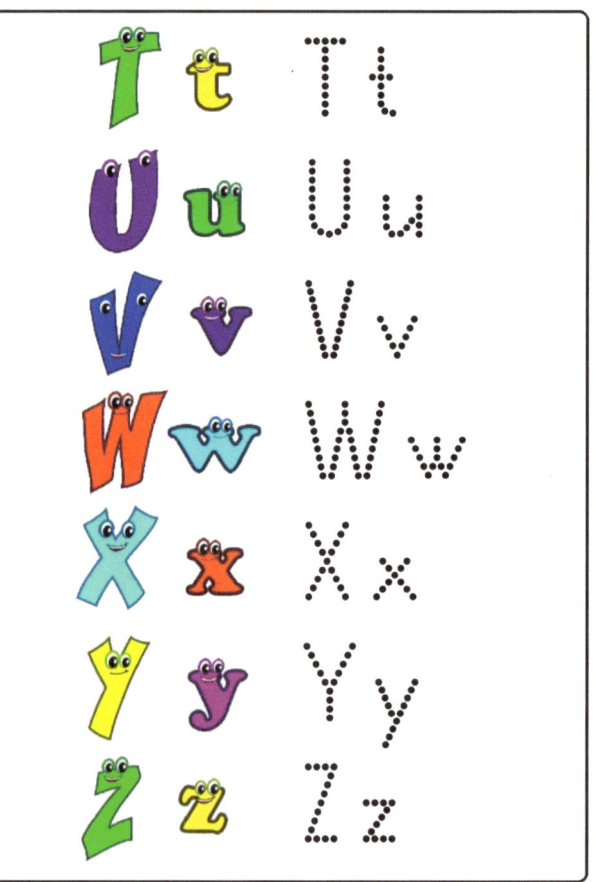

Level ONE Unit ONE
Let's play with the alphabet!

Sing the alphabet song!

How well did you do in this unit?
Write the CAN DO statement and assess yourself.
Write 3, 2, or 1
3 = VERY WELL
2 = WELL
1 = NOT SO WELL

I CAN...
_____
_____
_____
_____
_____
_____
_____

Level ONE Unit TWO
Let's play with numbers!

Learn the numbers

2.2 Dialogs

Level ONE Unit TWO
Let's play with numbers!

Practice the dialogs

Good morning! What's your name?
-Good morning! My name is Sandy.
How old are you Sandy?
-I am six years old.

Good morning! What's your name?
-Good morning! My name is Lucy.
How old are you Lucy?
-I am six years old.

Hello! What's your name?
-Hello! My name is Andy.
How old are you Andy?
-I am seven years old.

Hello! What's your name?
-Hello! My name is Tony.
How old are you Tony?
-I am seven years old.

Good morning! What's your name?
Good morning! My name is _____.
How old are you _____?
I am _____ years old.

16

Level ONE Unit TWO
Let's play with numbers!

2.3 Reading

Welcome to school

Miss Patty welcomes us
to school every day.
Miss Patty asks: How old are you?
I am 6 years old, answers Sandy.
I am 7 years old, answers Tony.
I am 6 years old, answers Lucy.
I am 7 years old, answers Andy.
We are all in first grade.
I love school!

Complete the sentences

1. Sandy is _____ years old.
    four   five   six
2. Tony is _____ years old.
    seven   six   three
3. Lucy is _____ years old.
    two   three   six
4. Andy is _____ years old.
    one   seven   eight
5. You are _____ years old.
    five   six   seven

2.4 Writing

Level ONE Unit TWO
Let's play with numbers!

Complete the reading with the words from the box below

Welcome to school

Miss Patty welcomes us to school every day.
Miss Patty asks: How old are you?
I am _____ years old, answers Sandy.
I am _____ years old, answers Tony.
I am _____ years old, answers Lucy.
I am _____ years old, answers Andy.
I am _____ years old, I answer.
We are all in first grade.
I love school!

one • two • three • four • five • six
seven • eight • nine • ten

Write the words. Say them aloud.

1 one	5 five	9 nine
2 two	6 six	10 ten
3 three	7 seven	
4 four	8 eight	

18

Level ONE Unit TWO
Let's play with numbers!

2.5 Language in use

Match the numbers with their name

eight	1
five	2
four	3
nine	4
one	5
seven	6
six	7
ten	8
three	9
two	10

Complete the numbers

e __ gh __
f __ v __
f __ __ r
ni __ __
__ n __
__ __ ven
si __
te __
thr __ __
t __ o

Sing the song

This old man

This old man, he played one,
He played knick-knack on my thumb;
**** With a knick-knack paddywhack,
Give a dog a bone,
This old man came rolling home.**
This old man, he played two,
He played knick-knack on my shoe;
** (repeat)
This old man, he played three,
He played knick-knack on my knee;
** (repeat)
This old man, he played four,
He played knick-knack on my door;
** (repeat)
This old man, he played five,
He played knick-knack on my hive;
** (repeat)

This old man, he played six,
He played knick-knack on my sticks;
** (repeat)
This old man, he played seven,
He played knick-knack up in Heaven;
** (repeat)
This old man, he played eight,
He played knick-knack on my gate;
** (repeat)
This old man, he played nine,
He played knick-knack on my spine;
** (repeat)
This old man, he played ten,
He played knick-knack once again;
** (repeat)

How well did you do in this unit?
Write the CAN DO statement and assess yourself.
Write 3, 2, or 1
3 = VERY WELL
2 = WELL
1 = NOT SO WELL

I CAN...
_____
_____
_____
_____
_____
_____
_____

Level ONE Unit THREE
Let's play with classroom language!

3.1 Vocabulary

Learn the classroom language

color

Open your book!

write

point

Sit down, please!

Be quiet, please!

Close your book!

Stand up, please!

listen

repeat

3.2 Dialogs

Level ONE Unit THREE
Let's play with classroom language!

Practice the dialogs

Lucy, open your book please!
- Yes, Miss Patty. Thank you.

Sandy, close your book please!
- Yes, Miss Patty. Thank you

Tony, be quiet please!
- Yes, Miss Patty Thank you.

Andy, stand up please!
- Yes, Miss Patty. Thank you.

Write the homework!
- Yes, Miss Patty Thank you.

Repeat after me!
- Yes, Miss Patty Thank you.

Color the picture!
- Yes, Miss Patty. Thank you.

Now you!

You: _____
Your classmate: _____
You: _____
Your classmate: _____

Level ONE Unit THREE
Let's play with classroom language!

Our English class

My friends and I are very happy in our English class.
We learn new words every day like:
listen, repeat, write, color and point.
We also learn new expressions like:
stand up, sit down, open your book and be quiet.
I am very happy in my English class
because I learn new things every day!
Thank you teacher!

Answer the questions

1. What words do you learn at school?
   a) one, two, three   b) listen, repeat, write
2. What expressions do you learn in your English class?
   a) stand up, sit down   b) five, six, seven
3. How do you feel in English class?
   a) angry   b) happy
4. What do you learn in class every day?
   a) new things   b) nothing

3.4 Writing

Level ONE Unit THREE
Let's play with classroom language!

Match the words with the correct image

listen

repeat

write

color

point

stand up

sit down

be quiet

Write the words. Say them aloud.

listen

repeat

write

color

point

stand up

sit down

be quiet

open

close

Level ONE Unit THREE
Let's play with classroom language!

3.5 Language in use

Complete the words. Match them with their image.

li__ te__

r__p__a__

wr__t__

c__l__r

poi__t

s__a__d up

sit __o__n

be __ui__t

ope__

__l__se

Say the rhyme:
Mary Had a Little Lamb

Mary had a little lamb,
It's fleece was white as snow;
And everywhere that Mary went,
The lamb was sure to go.

If followed her to school one day,
Which was against the rule;
It made the children laugh and play,
To see a lamb at school.

How well did you do in this unit?
Write the CAN DO statement and assess yourself.
Write 3, 2, or 1
3 = VERY WELL
2 = WELL
1 = NOT SO WELL

I CAN...
_____
_____
_____
_____
_____
_____
_____

Level ONE Unit FOUR
Let's play with the weather!

Learn the days of the week and the words for the weather

MY CALENDAR

1	2	3	4	5	6	7
Sunday	Monday	Tuesday	Wednesday	Thursday	Friday	Saturday

sunny	cloudy	snowy	windy
Sunday	Monday	Tuesday	Wednesday

rainy	sunny	cloudy
Thursday	Friday	Saturday

4.2 Dialogs

Level ONE Unit FOUR
Let's play with the weather!

Practice the dialogs

What day is today?
-Today is Monday.
How is the weather?
-It is cloudy.

Monday

What day is today?
-Today is Thursday.
How is the weather?
-It is rainy.

Thursday

What day is today?
-Today is Tuesday.
How is the weather?
-It is snowy.

Tuesday

What day is today?
-Today is Friday.
How is the weather?
-It is sunny.

Friday

What day is today?
-Today is Wednesday.
How is the weather?
-It is windy.

Wednesday

Now you!

What day is today?
Today is _____.
How is the weather?
It is _____.

Level ONE Unit FOUR
Let's play with the weather!

4.3 Reading

Beautiful weather

This week we see beautiful weather on our calendar every day.
On Sunday, it is sunny.
On Monday, it is cloudy.
On Tuesday, it is snowy.
On Wednesday, it is windy.
On Thursday, it is rainy.

Our calendar looks beautiful!

Answer the questions

How is the weather on Sunday?
a) sunny   b) snowy   c) cloudy

How is the weather on Monday?
a) snowy   b) cloudy   c) windy

How is the weather on Tuesday?
a) rainy   b) cloudy   c) snowy

How is the weather on Wednesday?
a) sunny   b) windy   c) rainy

Answer the questions with the correct days

1. What day is it sunny?
   _____.

2. What day is it cloudy?
   _____.

3. What day is it rainy?
   _____.

4. What day is it snowy?
   _____.

4.4 Writing

Level ONE Unit FOUR
Let's play with the weather!

Complete the reading with words from the box below. You may write them in any order you wish.

> Beautiful weather
>
> This week every day we see beautiful weather on our calendar.
>
> On _____, it is _____.
>
> On _____, it is _____.
>
> On _____, it is _____.
>
> Our calendar looks beautiful!

Monday • Tuesday • Wednesday • Thursday • Friday
sunny • cloudy • windy • rainy • snowy

Write the words. Say them aloud.

Sunday	Thursday	windy
Monday	Friday	rainy
Tuesday	sunny	snowy
Wednesday	cloudy	

Level ONE Unit FOUR
Let's play with the weather!

4.5 Language in use

We use **IS** for the singular form of the verb **to BE**

The days of the week take a capital letter at the beginning of the word.

We must put a **question mark** at the end of the question **(?)**

Choose the correct letter

a) ____ onday
    M   m

b) ____ uesday
    t   T

c) ____ ednesday
    W   w

d) ____ unday
    s   S

e) ____ riday
    F   f

Complete the sentences

1. Today ____ ____ onday.
   is   M   m

2. It ____ ____ unny.
   S   s   is

3. What day ____ today ____
   ?   is   T

4. Today ____ ____ riday.
   F   f   is

5. It ____ ____ indy.
   W   is   w

6. How ____ the weather ____
   W   ?   is

How well did you do in this unit?
Write the CAN DO statement and assess yourself.
Write 3, 2, or 1
3 = VERY WELL
2 = WELL
1 = NOT SO WELL

I CAN...
_____
_____
_____
_____
_____
_____
_____

Level ONE Unit FIVE
Let's play at school!

Learn the places in your school

Level ONE Unit FIVE
Let's play at school!

Practice the dialogs

What is this?
-This is the classroom.

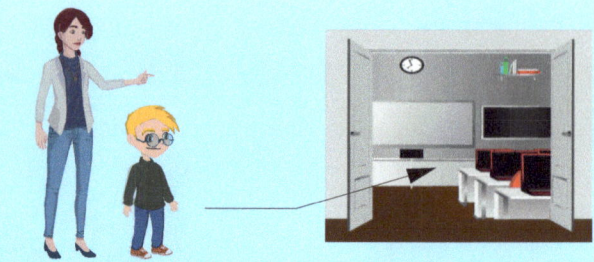

What is that?
-That is the computer room.

What is this?
-This is the music room.

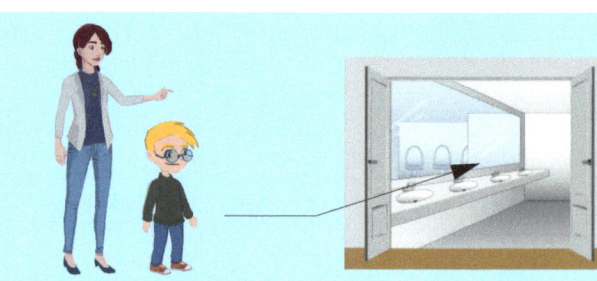

What is that?
-That is the restroom.

What is this?
-This is the cafeteria.

What is that?
-That is the library.

What is this?
-This is the office.

What is that/this?
-That/this is the _____.

Level ONE Unit FIVE
Let's play at school!

5.3 Reading

Welcome to school

 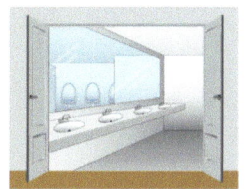

This is our beautiful school:
This is the classroom and
that is the restroom.
This is the music room and
That is the library.
This is the cafeteria and
that is the theater.
This is the computer room and
that is the school yard.
This is the office.
Our school is beautiful, I love our school!

Choose the correct answer

What is this?
- This is the computer room
- This is the classroom.
- This is the restroom.

What is that?
- That is the library.
- That is the music room.
- That is the classroom.

What is this?
- This is the office.
- This is the school yard.
- This is the restroom.

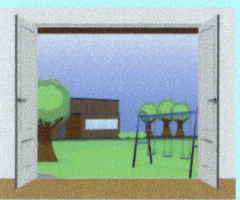

35

5.4 Writing

Level ONE Unit FIVE
Let's play at school!

Complete the reading with the words from the box below

This is our beautiful school:
This is the _____ and that is the _____.
This is the _____ and that is the _____.
This is the _____ and that is the _____.
This is the _____ and that is the _____.
This is the _____.
Our school is beautiful, I love our school!

restroom • computer room • office • cafeteria
school yard • music room • classroom • theater • library

Write the words. Say them aloud.

restroom
computer room
office
cafeteria
school yard

music room
classroom
theater
library

Level ONE Unit FIVE
Let's play at school!

5.5 Language in use

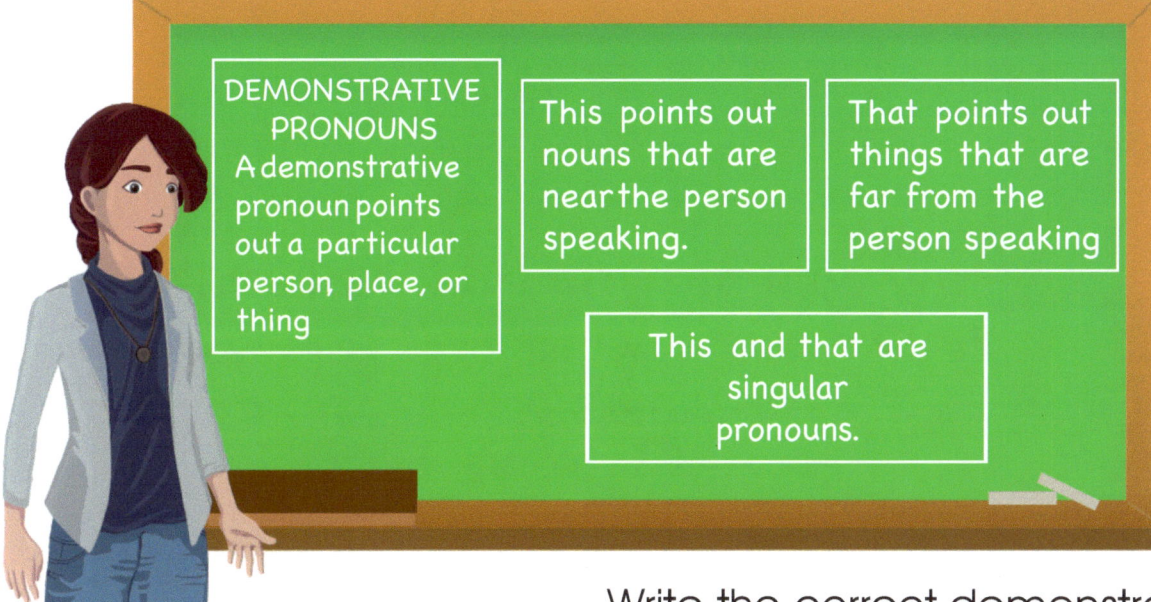

DEMONSTRATIVE PRONOUNS
A demonstrative pronoun points out a particular person, place, or thing

This points out nouns that are near the person speaking.

That points out things that are far from the person speaking

This and that are singular pronouns.

Choose the correct picture

That is the restroom.
☐   ☐

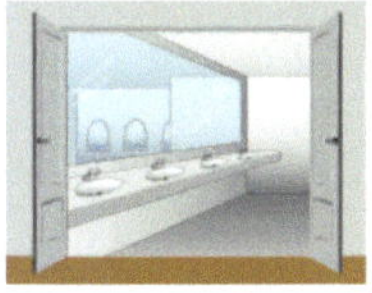

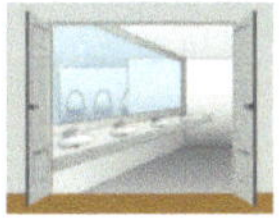

This is the office.
☐   ☐

That is the cafeteria.
☐   ☐

This is the music room.
☐   ☐

Write the correct demonstrative pronoun

_____
this   that

_____
this   that

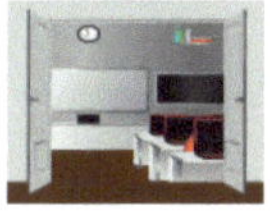

_____
this   that

_____
this   that

_____
this   that

How well did you do in this unit?
Write the CAN DO statement and assess yourself.
Write 3, 2, or 1
3 = VERY WELL
2 = WELL
1 = NOT SO WELL

I CAN...
_____
_____
_____
_____
_____
_____
_____

Level ONE Unit SIX
Let's play in the classroom!

Learn the objects in your classroom

6.2 Dialogs

Practice the dialogs

Is this the desk?
-Yes, that is the desk.

Is this the bookshelf?
-Yes, that is the bookshelf.

Is this the book?
-Yes, that is the book.

 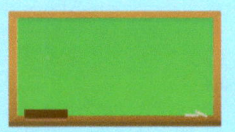 

Is this the board?
-Yes, that is the board.

Is this a _____?
Yes, that is a _____.

Level ONE Unit SIX
Let's play in the classroom!

Welcome to our classroom

Welcome to our classroom!!

Miss Patty welcomes us to our classroom, she shows us many things.

Look! This is the board and that is the bookshelf.
This is the chair and that is the clock.
This is the desk and that is the door.
That is the map and this is the table.
That is the wall and this is the window.
I love our classroom!

Choose the correct sentence

What is this?
a) This is the bookshelf
b) This is the board

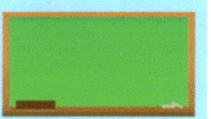

What is that?
a) That is the bookshelf
b) That is the board

What is this?
a) This is the desk
b) This is the chair

Choose the correct picture.

Is this the chair?
- Yes, that is the chair.

Is this the board?
- Yes, that is the board.

  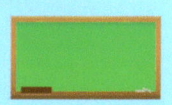

Is this the desk?
- Yes, that is the desk.

 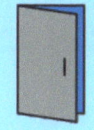 

6.4 Writing

Level ONE Unit SIX
Let's play in the classroom!

Complete the reading with the words from the box below

Welcome to our classroom

Miss Patty welcomes us to our classroom, she shows us many things.

Look! This is the _____ and that is the _____.
This is the _____ and that is the _____.
This is the _____ and that is the _____.
That is the _____ and this is the _____.
That is the _____ and this is the _____.

I love our classroom!

board • bookshelf • chair • clock • desk • door
map • table • wall • window

Write the words. Say them aloud.

board   desk   table
chair   door   wall
clock   map   window

Level ONE Unit SIX
Let's play in the classroom!

6.5 Language in use

To make a question with the verb BE the subject and the verb change positions.
Affirmative: This is the map.
Interrogative: Is this the map?

To give a short affirmative answer we always use:
Yes, (comma) **it is.** (period)
We do not use a contracted form for the short answer.
Yes, it's.

Change the sentences into questions

1. This is the bookshelf.
   _____?

2. This is the board.
   _____?

3. This is the desk.
   _____?

4. This is the chair.
   _____?

5. This is the map.
   _____?

Choose the correct short answer

Is this the chair?
a) Yes this is. b) Yes, it is. c) Yes it is

Is this the wall?
a) Yes, it is. b) Yes, is it? c) Yes this is.

Is this the clock?
a) Yes, it's.   b) Yes, it is.   c) Yes is it.

Is this the bookshelf?
a) Yes, it's   b) Yes, this is.   c) Yes, it is.

Is this the table?
a) Yes, it is.   b) Yes, it's.   c) Yes, is this.

43

How well did you do in this unit?
Write the CAN DO statement and assess yourself.
Write 3, 2, or 1
3 = VERY WELL
2 = WELL
1 = NOT SO WELL

I CAN...
_____
_____
_____
_____
_____
_____
_____

Level ONE Unit SEVEN
Let's play with school objects!

7.1 Vocabulary

Learn the school objects in your backpack

- book
- scissors
- pencil
- notebook
- eraser
- sharpener
- ruler
- crayon
- marker
- pen

7.2 Dialogs

Level ONE Unit SEVEN
Let's play with school objects!

Practice the dialogs

Where is the pen?
- It is on the chair.

Where is the pencil?
- It is under the table.

Where is the crayon?
- It is in the school bag.

Where is the book?
- It is on the bookshelf.

Where is the sharpener?
- It is under the chair.

Now you!

Where is the_____?
It is on the_____.

Level ONE Unit SEVEN
Let's play with school objects!

7.3 Reading

This is my school bag

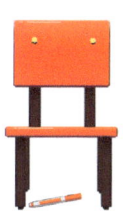

My school bag is beautiful.
The pencil is in the bag.
The pen is in the bag too.
The crayon is in the bag and
the notebook is also in the bag.
Oops! Where is the ruler?
- It is on the desk.
Oh! Where is the marker?
- It is under the chair.
Oh no! Where is the book?
- It is on the bookshelf.
I love my school bag!

Choose the correct answer

Where is the book?
❑ on the bag   ❑ on the desk   ❑ on the bookshelf

Where is the marker?
❑ on the desk   ❑ on the bag   ❑ under the chair

Where is the crayon?
❑ in the bag   ❑ on the desk   ❑ on the chair

Choose the correct picture

Where is the pencil?    ❑    ❑    ❑

Where is the notebook?   ❑    ❑    ❑

Where is the ruler?    ❑    ❑   ❑

7.4 Writing

Level ONE Unit SEVEN
Let's play with school objects!

Complete the reading with the words from the box below

My school bag is beautiful
The pencil is ___ the bag.
The pen is in the bag too.
The crayon is in the bag and the notebook is also in the bag.
Oops! Where is the _____?
-It is under the desk.
Oh! Where is the _____?
-It is _____ the chair.
Oh no! Where is the _____?
-It is _____ the bookshelf.
I love my school bag!

in • on • under • pen • pencil • crayon • ruler • sharpener
• eraser • book • notebook • marker • scissors

Write the words. Say them aloud.

pen	eraser
pencil	book
crayon	notebook
ruler	marker
sharpener	scissors

Level ONE Unit SEVEN
Let's play with school objects!

7.5
Language in use

A **pronoun** is a word that takes the place of a noun.
The pronoun **IT** takes the place of a singular object.
The book is on the bookshelf.
It is on the bookshelf.

The prepositions **ON, IN, UNDER**
show the location of nouns.

The bag is on the chair

The bag is under the chair

The ruler is in the bag

Look at the pictures and write the missing words

Where is the sharpener?
-It is _____ the chair.

Where is the eraser?
-It is _____ the board.

Where is the book?
-It is _____ the bookshelf.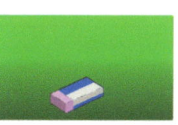

Complete the sentences

Where is the ruler?
-It is _____ the desk.
this   on   table

Where is the marker?
-_____ is on the chair.
the   it   is

Where is the book?
-It _____ on the bookshelf.

49

How well did you do in this unit?

Write the CAN DO statement and assess yourself.

Write 3, 2, or 1

3 = VERY WELL

2 = WELL

1 = NOT SO WELL

I CAN...

_____

_____

_____

_____

_____

_____

Level ONE Unit EIGHT
Let's play colors and shapes!

Learn the colors and shapes

Learning colors

red blue yellow green orange

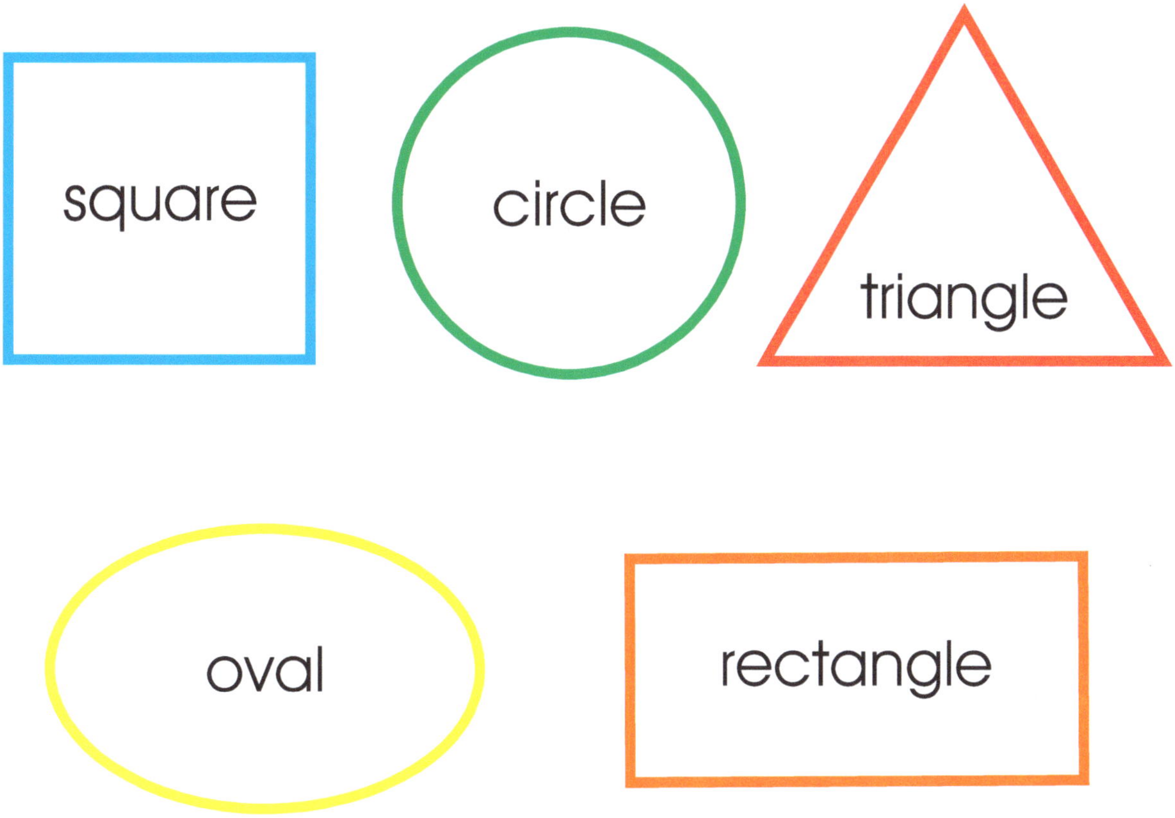

square circle triangle

oval rectangle

8.2 Dialogs

Level ONE Unit EIGHT
Let's play colors and shapes!

Practice the dialogs

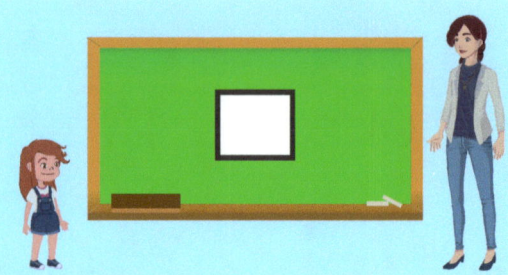
Is this a yellow square?
-No it isn't yellow square.
It's a green square.

Is this a green oval?
-No it isn't a green oval.
-It is a yellow oval.

Is this a yellow rectangle?
-No, it isn't a yellow rectangle.
-It is an orange rectangle.

Is this a blue triangle?
-No, it isn't a blue triangle.
-It is a red triangle.

Is this a/an _____ _____?
No, it isn't a/an _____ _____.
It is a/an _____ _____.

Level ONE Unit EIGHT
Let's play colors and shapes!

Colors and shapes

Miss Patty teaches us about colors and shapes today.
Now I know, this is isn't a red circle and it isn't a blue circle.
It is a yellow circle!
This isn't a red square and it isn't blue square. It is a green square!
This isn't a red rectangle and it isn't a blue rectangle.
It is an orange rectangle!
This isn't a blue triangle and it isn't a yellow triangle.
It is a red triangle!
This isn't a red oval and it isn't an orange oval. It is a blue oval!
What is your favorite color and shape?
I love colors and shapes!

Choose the correct answer

What color is the circle?
❏ red   ❏ blue   ❏ yellow

What color is the square?
❏ red   ❏ green   ❏ blue

What color is the rectangle?
❏ orange   ❏ blue   ❏ red

What color is the triangle?
❏ blue   ❏ red   ❏ yellow

What color is the oval?
❏ blue   ❏ orange   ❏ red

Based on the reading answer true or false

1. It is a yellow circle.
   true ❏   false ❏

2. It is an orange square
   true ❏   false ❏

3. It is a red rectangle
   true ❏   false ❏

4. It is green triangle
   true ❏   false ❏

5. It is blue oval
   true ❏   false ❏

8.4 Writing

Level ONE Unit EIGHT
Let's play colors and shapes!

Complete the reading with the words from the box below

This is my school bag!
Miss Patty today teaches us about colors and shapes.

Now, I know this isn't a red (shape) _____
and it isn't a blue (shape) _____ . It is a yellow (shape) _____ !
This isn't a (color) _____ square
and it isn't (color) _____ square. It is a (color) _____ square!
This isn't a blue (shape) _____
and it isn't a yellow (shape) _____ . It is a red (shape) _____ !
This isn't a (color) _____ oval
and it isn't a (color) _____ oval. It is a (color) _____ oval!

What is your favorite color and shape?
I love colors and shapes!

---

red • yellow • green • blue • orange
square • circle • triangle • rectangle • oval

Write the words. Say them aloud.

red   orange   triangle

blue   square   oval

yellow   circle

green   rectangle

Level ONE Unit EIGHT
Let's play colors and shapes!

8.5 Language in use

Adjectives are words that describe.
Colors describe nouns.
This is a red circle.
Adjectives are not used in a plural form.

The negative form of the verb BE for the singular form: is+not.
It can also be used in its contracted form: isn't.

We give a short negative answer:
No, (comma) it isn't. (period)

Choose the correct answer

1. Is this a yellow circle?
   Yes, it is.
   No, it isn't.
   No it is.
2. Is this a blue rectangle?
   No, it isn't.
   Yes, it is.
   No, it is.
3. Is this a red triangle?
   No, it is.
   Yes, it is.
   No, it isn't.
4. Is this an orange square?
   No it isn't
   No, it isn't.
   Yes, it is.

Order the sentences

1. This _____ a _____ _____.
   yellow   is   square

2. _____ is _____ a _____ triangle.
   red   this   not

3. It _____ a _____ _____.
   rectangle   isn't   blue

4. _____ isn't _____ orange _____.
   an   circle   it

5. _____ is _____ _____ oval.
   That   green   a

55

How well did you do in this unit?
Write the CAN DO statement and assess yourself.
Write 3, 2, or 1
3 = VERY WELL
2 = WELL
1 = NOT SO WELL

I CAN...
___
___
___
___
___
___
___

Level ONE Unit NINE
Let's play with my family!

9.1 Vocabulary

Learn the family members

Sandy

father   mother   sister   brother   baby   grandfather   grandmother

9.2 Dialogs

Level ONE Unit NINE
Let's play with my family!

Practice the dialogs

Who is this?
-This is my mother.

Who is this?
-This is my father.

Who is this?
-This is my grandmother.

Who is this?
-This is my grandfather.

Who is this?
-This is my sister.

Who is this?
-This is my brother.

Who is this?
-This is my baby brother.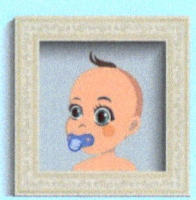

Who is this/that?
This/that is my_____

Level ONE Unit NINE
Let's play with my family!

This is my beautiful family

That is my father and this is my mother.
This is my brother and this is my sister.
That is my grandfather and that is my grandmother.
Oh yes! That is my baby brother.
I love my family!

Re-order the words

t e r h m o

e r h t a f

b o h r t e

s r i e s t

y a b b

r g e r h a t n a d f

Choose the correct family member

This is my mother
☐ ☐ ☐

This is my sister
☐ ☐ ☐

This is my father
☐ ☐ ☐

This is my baby brother
☐ ☐ ☐

9.4 Writing

Level ONE Unit NINE
Let's play with my family!

Complete the reading with the words from the box below

This is my beautiful family!
This is my _____ and that is my _____.
This is my _____ and that is my _____.
This is my _____ and that is my _____. Oh yes!
And that is my _____.

I love my family!

mother • father • grandmother • grandfather
brother • sister • baby brother

Write the words. Say them aloud.

brother	brother
father	father
grandfather	grandfather
grandmother	grandmother
mother	mother
sister	sister

Level ONE Unit NINE
Let's play with my family!

9.5 Language in use

Possessive adjectives are used to show possession of something. My book = ownership

When we refer to people it refers to relationship.

My mother = relationship

The possessive adjective for the 1st person "I" is "MY"

Who asks for a person.

Order the sentences

1. _____ _____ _____ ?
   is   Who   that

2. That _____ _____ _____.
   father   my   is

3. _____ _____ my _____.
   is   sister   this

4. _____ is _____ ?
   Who   that

5. _____ _____ _____ grandmother.
   This   my   is

Write the correct sentence

_____ _____ _____ _____.

_____ _____ _____ _____.

_____ _____ _____ _____.

_____ _____ _____ _____.

_____ _____ _____ _____.

This is my grandfather.
This is my father.
This is my grandmother.
This is my sister.
This is my mother.

How well did you do in this unit?
Write the CAN DO statement and assess yourself.
Write 3, 2, or 1
3 = VERY WELL
2 = WELL
1 = NOT SO WELL

I CAN...
_____
_____
_____
_____
_____
_____
_____

Level ONE Unit TEN
Let's play at home!

Learn the rooms in the home

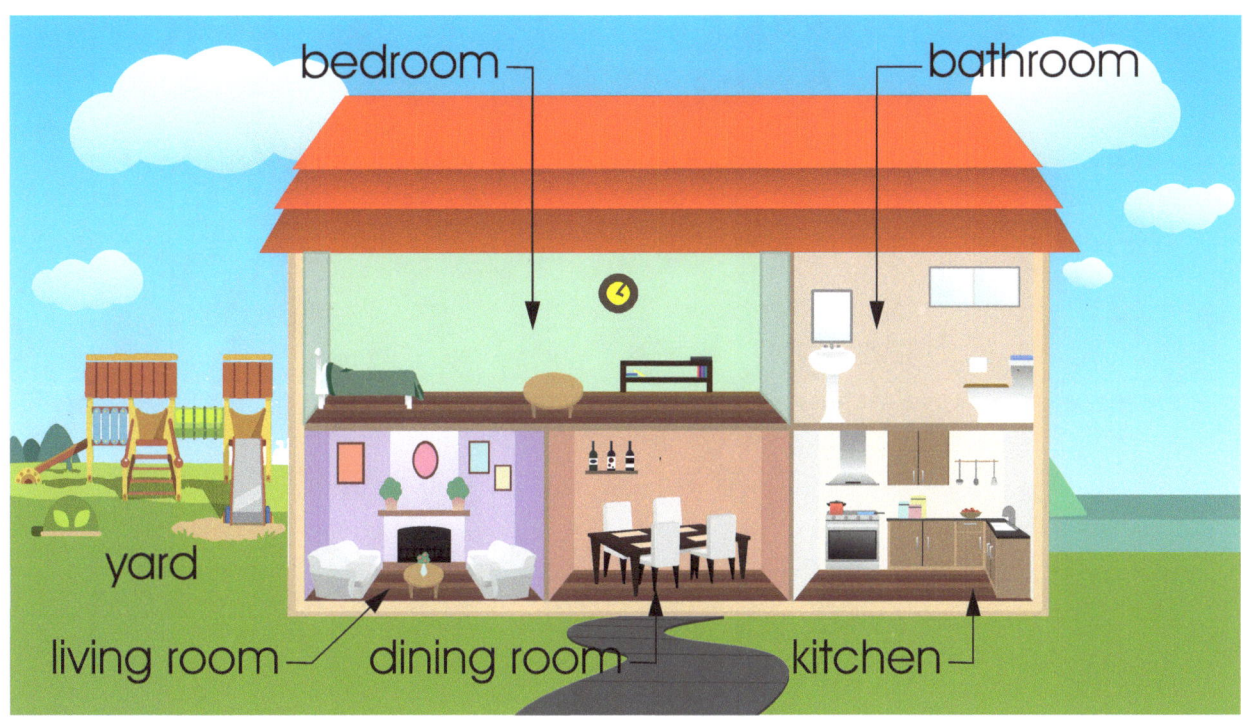

10.2 Dialogs

Level ONE Unit TEN
Let's play at home!

Practice the dialogs

Is this the kitchen?
-No, it isn't. It's the dining room.

Is this the bedroom?
-No, it isn't. It's the living room.

Is this the dining room?
-No, it isn't. It's the kitchen.

Is this the bathroom?
-No, it isn't. It's the bedroom.

Is this the _____?
No, it isn't. It's the _____.

Level ONE Unit TEN
Let's play at home!

10.3 Reading

Welcome to my home!

This is the kitchen, it is a yellow kitchen.
This is the bedroom, it is a blue bedroom.
This is the bathroom, it is a green bathroom.
This is the living room; it is a red living room.
This is the yard. It is many colors.
I love my home!

Re-order the sentences

____ _____ ____ green.
The   is   bathroom

_____ _____ the _____ .
This   yard   is

That ____ ____ _____ .
is   the   kitchen

_____ _____ is _____ .
blue   the   bedroom.

Choose the correct color

The kitchen is:
☐ green ☐ yellow ☐ blue

The bedroom is:
☐ red ☐ blue ☐ orange

The bathroom is:
☐ blue ☐ orange ☐ green

The living room is:
☐ red ☐ orange ☐ yellow

10.4 Writing

Level ONE Unit TEN
Let's play at home!

Complete the reading with the words from the box below

Welcome to my home

This is the kitchen, it is a _____ (color) kitchen.

This is the yard, it is a _____ (color) yard.

This is the bedroom, it is a _____ (color) bedroom.

This is the living room, it is a _____ (color) living room.

I love my home!

red • blue • yellow • orange • green

Write the words. Say them aloud.

kitchen   living room
bathroom   yard
bedroom   dining room

Level ONE Unit TEN
Let's play at home!

10.5 Language in use

Where asks for a place
Where is the kitchen?

Is this the kitchen?
No, it isn't. It's the dining room.

We can give a short negative answer and then complement with additional information.

We can use colors to describe our room.
This is a yellow kitchen.

Complete the sentences

Is this a yellow kitchen?
-No, _____ isn't.
-It's a green _____.

Is this a green bathroom?
-No, it _____.
-It's a _____ bathroom.

Where _____ the dining room?
_____ is the yard?
Where is the _____?

bedroom • where
is • it • blue • isn't

Answer the questions

Is this the bedroom?
-No, it isn't.
-It's the _____.

Is this the bathroom?
-No, it isn't.
-It's the _____.

Is this the dining room?
-No, it isn't.
-It's the _____.

Is this the kitchen?
-No, it isn't.
-It's the _____.

Is this the dining room?
-No, it isn't.
-It's the _____.

How well did you do in this unit?
Write the CAN DO statement and assess yourself.
Write 3, 2, or 1
3 = VERY WELL
2 = WELL
1 = NOT SO WELL

I CAN...
_____
_____
_____
_____
_____
_____
_____

Level ONE Unit ELEVEN
Let's play with family at home!

Learn the family and the rooms in the home

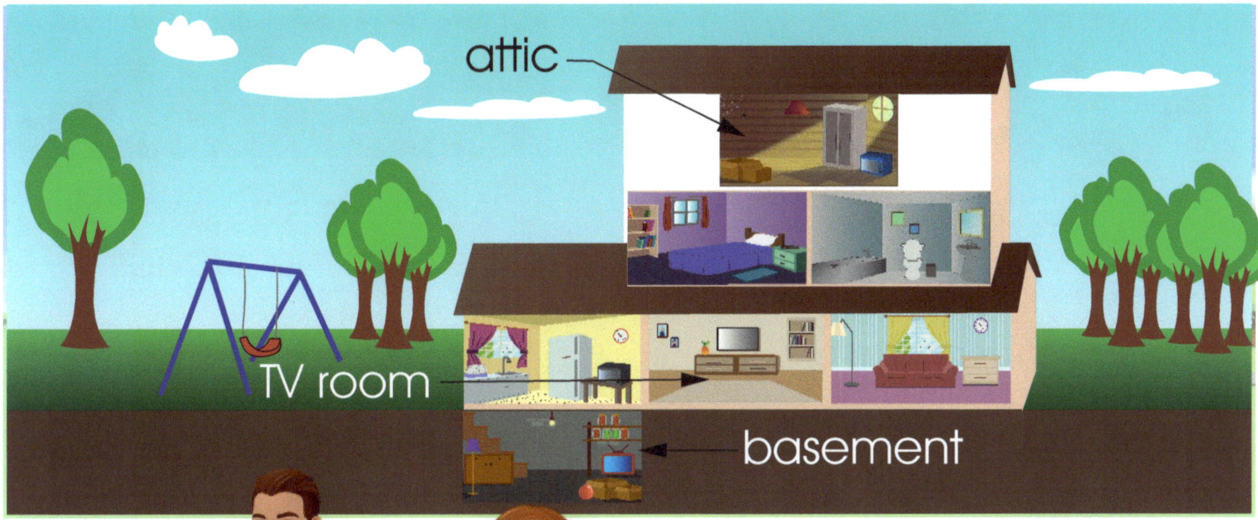

attic

TV room

basement

uncle   aunt   cousin   cousin

11.2 Dialogs

Level ONE Unit ELEVEN
Let's play with family at home!

Practice the dialogs

Where is uncle?
-He is in the TV room.

Where is aunt?
-She is in bedroom.

Where is aunt?
-She is in the attic.

Where is cousin Tim?
-He is in the kitchen.

Where is cousin Mary?
-She is in the basement.

Where is mother?
-She is in the bedroom.

Where is grandmother?
-She is in the living room.

Now you!

Where is _____?
-He/she is in the _____.

Level ONE Unit ELEVEN
Let's play with family at home!

11.3
Reading

This is my family's home!

My father is in the TV room and
my mother is in the attic.
My cousin Mary is in the basement and
my brother is in the kitchen.
My aunt is in the bedroom and
uncle is in the living room.
Oh! Where is grandmother?
She is in the yard!.
I love my family's home!

Answer the questions

Where is grandmother?
❏ TV room ❏ attic ❏ yard

Where is uncle?
❏ bedroom ❏ basement
❏ living room

Where is aunt?
❏ bedroom ❏ kitchen ❏ yard

Where is brother?
❏ attic ❏ TV room ❏ kitchen

Where is cousin Mary?
❏ kitchen ❏ yard ❏ basement

Answer the questions

Is father in the yard?
-No, he isn't. He's in the
_____.

Is uncle in the bathroom?
-No, he isn't. He's in the
_____.

Is aunt in the dining room?
No, she isn't. She's in the
_____.

11.4 Writing

Level ONE Unit ELEVEN
Let's play with family at home!

Complete the reading with the words from the box below

This is my family's home!

My _____ is in the _____ and my _____ is in the _____ .

My _____ is in the _____ and my _____ is in the _____ .

My _____ is in the _____ and my _____ is in the _____ .

I love my family's home!

---

uncle • aunt • cousin • mother • father • grandmother
grandfather • brother • sister • kitchen • living room
dining room • bathroom • bedroom • basement • attic
yard • TV room

Write the words. Say them aloud.

uncle	bedroom	living room
aunt	kitchen	bathroom
cousin	basement	
attic	TV room	

Level ONE Unit ELEVEN
Let's play with family at home!

11.5 Language in use

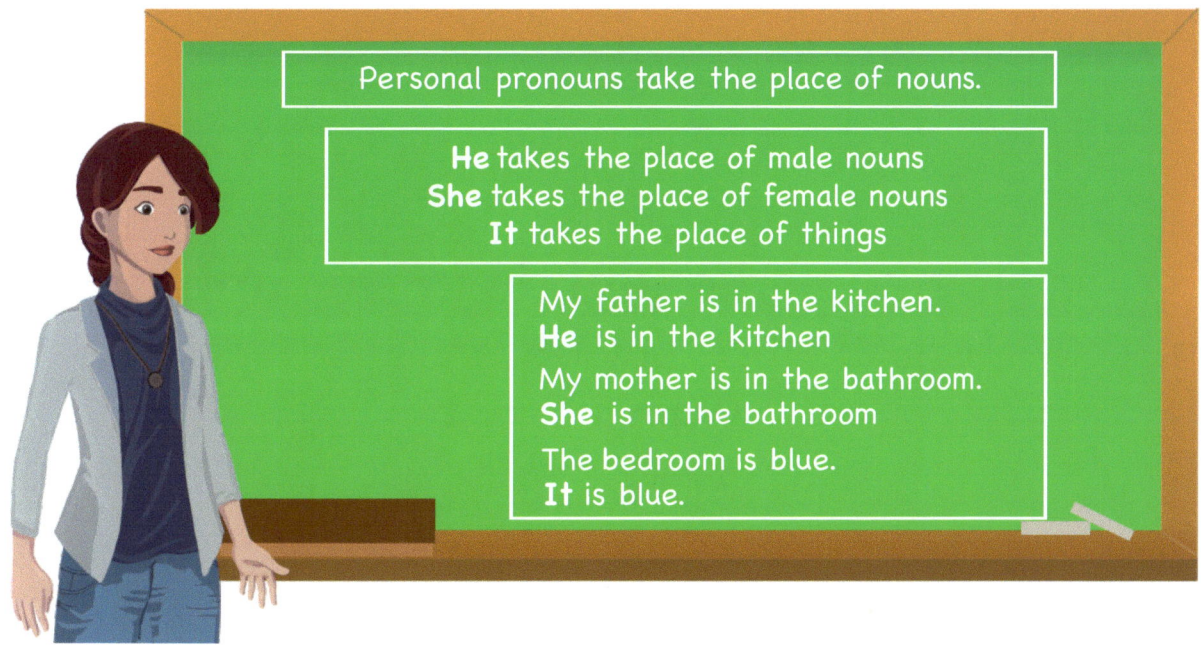

Personal pronouns take the place of nouns.

He takes the place of male nouns
She takes the place of female nouns
It takes the place of things

My father is in the kitchen.
He is in the kitchen
My mother is in the bathroom.
She is in the bathroom
The bedroom is blue.
It is blue.

Write the correct pronoun

(Mother)
_____ is in the attic.

(Father)
_____ is in the kitchen.

(The bedroom)
_____ is blue.

(Uncle Tim)
_____ is in the bathroom.

(Cousin Mary)
_____ is in the dining room.

(The kitchen)
_____ is yellow.

Choose the correct pronoun

<u>Father</u> is in the TV room.
❑ He   ❑ She   ❑ It

<u>The living room</u> is red.
❑ He   ❑ She   ❑ It

<u>Mother</u> is in the attic.
❑ He   ❑ She   ❑ It

<u>Cousin Mary</u> is in the basement.
❑ He   ❑ She   ❑ It

<u>Brother</u> is in the kitchen.
❑ He   ❑ She   ❑ It

<u>The kitchen</u> is yellow.
❑ He   ❑ She   ❑ It

How well did you do in this unit?
Write the CAN DO statement and assess yourself.
Write 3, 2, or 1
3 = VERY WELL
2 = WELL
1 = NOT SO WELL

I CAN...
_____
_____
_____
_____
_____
_____
_____

Level ONE Unit TWELVE
Let's play with emotions!

Learn the emotions

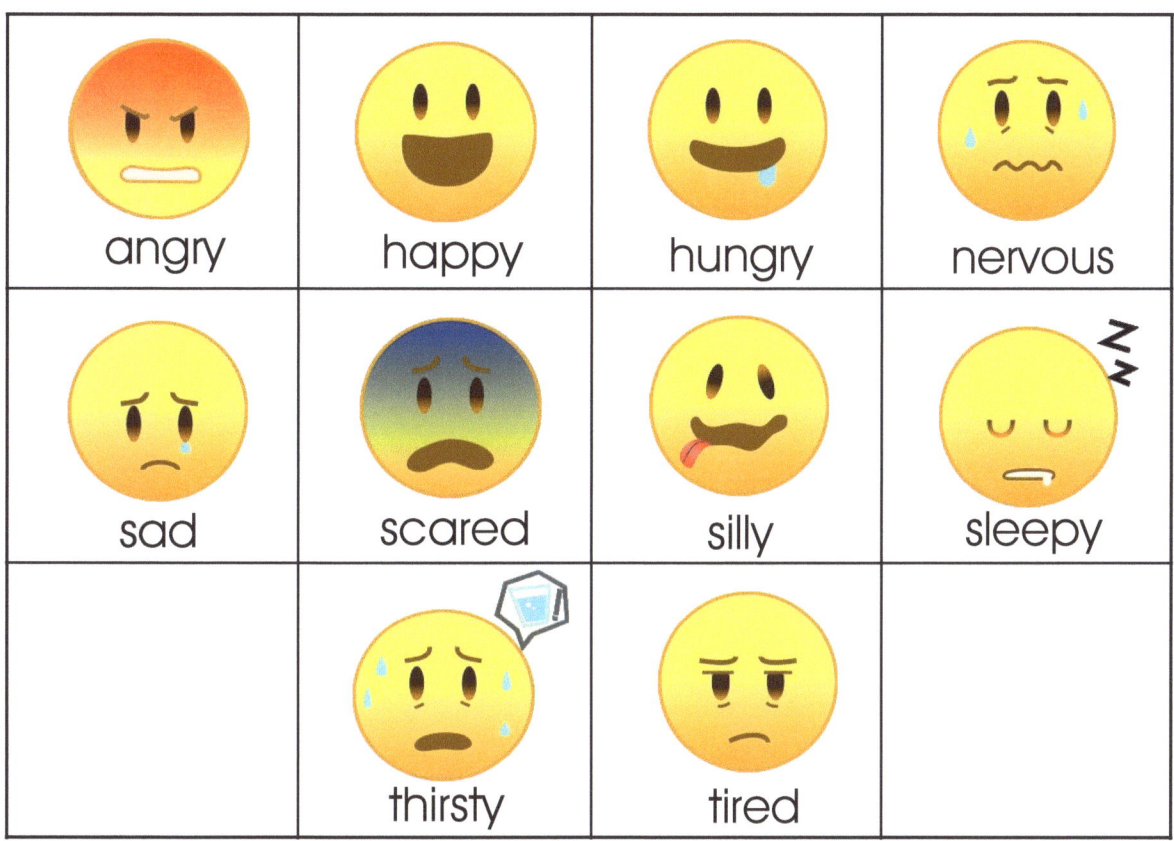

Find the emotions

L	N	L	W	X	G	I	J	I	I
C	D	T	S	Y	R	G	N	A	Y
N	E	H	I	R	Y	N	Z	O	P
N	R	I	L	G	P	E	Z	V	E
D	I	R	L	N	P	R	O	V	E
E	T	S	Y	U	A	V	R	H	L
R	T	T	R	H	H	O	D	A	S
A	U	Y	Y	R	H	U	P	X	V
C	N	I	C	O	Z	S	F	G	A
S	H	V	X	P	A	U	Y	O	S

ANGRY
HAPPY
HUNGRY
NERVOUS
SAD
SCARED
SILLY
SLEEPY
THIRSTY
TIRED

12.2 Dialogs

Level ONE Unit TWELVE
Let's play with emotions!

Practice the dialogs

Is father sad?
-No, he isn't. He's happy.

Is grandmother sleepy?
-No, she isn't. She's sad.

Is sister angry?
-No, she isn't. She's scared.

Is uncle hungry?
-No, he isn't. He's thirsty.

Is mother angry?
-No, she isn't. She's nervous.

Is aunt sleepy?
-No, she isn't. She's hungry

Is brother silly?
-No, he isn't. He's tired.

Now you!

Is _____ _____?
-No, he/she isn't.
He/she is _____.

Level ONE Unit TWELVE
Let's play with emotions!

How is your family today?

My father is sleepy today.
My mother is tired today.
My sister is thirsty today.
My brother is silly today.
My uncle is angry today.
My aunt is hungry today.
I love my family,
I am very happy today!

Match the questions with the correct emotion

- How is father today?

- How is mother today?

- How is sister today?

- How is brother today?

- How is uncle today?

Answer the questions

1. How is father today?
   ☐ happy ☐ sleepy ☐ hungry

2. How is mother today?
   ☐ happy ☐ tired ☐ angry

3. How is sister today?
   ☐ thirsty ☐ sad ☐ sleepy

4. How is brother today?
   ☐ silly ☐ angry ☐ happy

5. How is uncle today?
   ☐ thirsty ☐ tired ☐ angry

12.4 Writing

Level ONE Unit TWELVE
Let's play with emotions!

Complete the reading with the words from the box below

How is your family today?

My father is _____ today.
My mother is _____ today.
My brother is _____ today.
My sister is _____ today.
My grandmother is _____ today.
And I am very _____ today.
I love my family!

angry • happy • hungry • nervous • sad
scared • silly • sleepy • thirsty • tired

Write the words. Say them aloud.

angry   scared
happy   silly
hungry   sleepy
nervous   thirsty
sad   tired

Level ONE Unit TWELVE
Let's play with emotions!

12.5 Language in use

Wh- questions request information
Who asks for a person.
Who is that?
Where asks for a place.
Where is mother?
What asks for thing or an action.
What is that?
How asks for a number or the way you feel.
How are you today?

Complete the questions with the correct Wh-question

Who • What • Where
What • How

_____ is your mother?
She's happy.

_____ is this?
It's a book.

_____ is your sister?
Nancy is my sister.

_____ is your father?
He's in the kitchen

_____ are you today?
I'm tired.

_____ is the pencil?
It's under the chair.

Choose the correct pronoun

Father is in the TV room.
❏ He ❏ She ❏ It

The living room is red.
❏ He ❏ She ❏ It

Mother is in the attic.
❏ He ❏ She ❏ It

Cousin Mary is in the basement.
❏ He ❏ She ❏ It

Brother is in the kitchen.
❏ He ❏ She ❏ It

The kitchen is yellow.
❏ He ❏ She ❏ It

How well did you do in this unit?
Write the CAN DO statement and assess yourself.
Write 3, 2, or 1
3 = VERY WELL
2 = WELL
1 = NOT SO WELL

I CAN...
_____
_____
_____
_____
_____
_____
_____

Level ONE Unit THIRTEEN
Let's play with clothes!

Learn the clothes

Find the clothes

S	S	E	A	N	Y	P	C	X	I	J	I
V	E	H	E	B	Q	A	M	O	E	C	C
O	S	S	O	H	J	N	I	A	E	W	S
X	U	J	S	E	I	T	N	Z	A	T	S
N	O	A	I	E	S	S	H	I	R	T	S
T	L	O	I	H	R	N	R	I	C	W	I
U	B	J	N	E	C	D	K	H	K	X	Z
P	U	B	Z	M	T	S	P	E	M	F	F
U	U	B	L	Y	W	P	R	T	B	J	T
T	R	X	F	J	G	E	R	T	D	S	M
S	E	O	H	S	S	I	N	N	E	T	W
D	T	Q	Y	P	T	W	V	P	X	A	Z

DRESSES

SKIRTS

BLOUSES

SHOES

SHIRTS

PANTS

JEANS

TENNIS SHOES

13.2 Dialogs

Level ONE Unit THIRTEEN
Let's play with clothes!

Practice the dialogs

Look! Those are my skirts.
-Are they green skirts?
No, they aren't.
They are red skirts.

Look! These are my jeans!
-Are they red jeans?
No, they aren't.
They are blue jeans.

Look! Those are my shirts!
-Are they blue shirts?
No, they aren't.
They are yellow shirts.

Look! These are my dresses.
-Are they red dresses?
No, they aren't.
They are orange dresses.

Look! Those are my blouses.
-Are they orange blouses?
No, they aren't.
They are green blouses.

Look! These are my pants.
-Are they blue pants?
No, they aren't.
They are green pants.

Look! Those are my shoes.
-Are they red shoes?
No, they aren't.
They are blue shoes.

Now you!

Look! These/those are my _____.
Are they _____ _____.
No, they aren't. They are _____ _____.

Level ONE Unit THIRTEEN
Let's play with clothes!

13.3 Reading

These are my favorite clothes!

These are my favorite clothes!
They are not blue blouses and they are not yellow skirts.
They are red dresses.
I love my red dresses!

These are my favorite clothes!
They are not orange shirts and they are not green pants.
They are blue jeans.
I love my blue jeans!

Complete the sentences

They _____ red dresses.
❑ is ❑ are ❑ am

They are _____ blue skirts.
❑ am ❑ is ❑ not

_____ are orange blouses.
❑ those ❑ it ❑ you

These are yellow _____.
❑ shirt ❑ blue ❑ shirts

_____ are not green pants.
❑ it ❑ she ❑ those

Answer the questions

What are Sandy's favorite clothes?
Are they blue blouses?
❑ Yes ❑ No
Are they yellow skirts?
❑ Yes ❑ No
Are they red dresses?
❑ Yes ❑ No

What are Andy's favorite clothes?
Are they orange shirts?
❑ Yes ❑ No
Are they green pants?
❑ Yes ❑ No
Are they blue jeans?
❑ Yes ❑ No

13.4 Writing

Level ONE Unit THIRTEEN
Let's play with clothes!

Complete the reading with the words from the box below

At my favorite store

These are my favorite clothes!
These are my favorite clothes!
They are not _____ _____ and
they are not _____ _____.
They are _____ _____.
I love my _____ _____!

dresses	shirts	red
skirts	pants	yellow
blouses	jeans	green
shoes	tennis shoes	blue
		orange

Write the words. Say them aloud.

dresses   pants
skirts   jeans
blouses   tennis
shoes   shoes
shirts

Level ONE Unit THIRTEEN
Let's play with clothes!

 13.5 Language in use

Plural Demonstrative Pronouns

We use THESE to talk about people or things near us.
We use THOSE to talk about people or things far from us.

We form the plural by adding 'S' to noun.
Skirt (singular) skirt+s = skirts (plural)

They is the personal pronoun for plurals.
The skirts are green. They are green.

Re-order the sentences

1. ____ ____ ____ ____ .
   socks they green are

2. ____ ____ ____ ____ .
   jeans aren't blue these

3. ____ ____ ____ ____ .
   are orange blouses those

4. ____ ____ ____ ____ .
   are they pants orange

5. ____ ____ ____ ____ .
   yellow shirts are they

Choose the correct word to complete the sentence

They are green _____.
☐ sock   ☐ socks

_____ are blue skirts.
☐ It   ☐ They

Those _____ red shoes.
☐ is   ☐ are

_____ are yellow jeans.
☐ These   ☐ This

_____ are orange dresses.
☐ Those   ☐ That

How well did you do in this unit?
Write the CAN DO statement and assess yourself.
Write 3, 2, or 1
3 = VERY WELL
2 = WELL
1 = NOT SO WELL

I CAN...
_____
_____
_____
_____
_____
_____
_____

Level ONE Unit FOURTEEN
Let's play at the store!

Describe the clothes

brown 
skirt

white 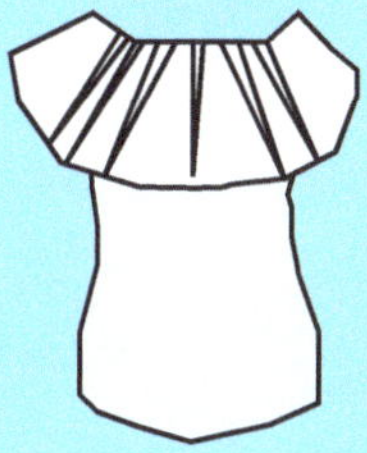
blouse

pink 
pants

black 
tennis shoes

purple 
shoes

14.2 Dialogs

Level ONE Unit FOURTEEN
Let's play at the store!

Practice the dialogs

Excuse me! Is there a pink blouse?
-No, there isn't.
-But there is a white blouse.
Oh, no! Thank you.
-You're welcome.

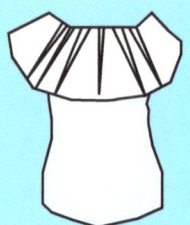

Excuse me! Is there a white pair of tennis shoes?
-No, there isn't.
-But there is a black pair of tennis shoes.
Oh, no! Thank you.
-You're welcome.

Excuse me! Is there a purple skirt?
-No, there isn't.
-But there is a brown skirt.
Oh, no! Thank you.
-You're welcome.

Excuse me! Is there a black pair of shoes?
-No, there isn't.
-But there is a purple pair of shoes.
Oh, no! Thank you.
-You're welcome.

Excuse me!
Is there a _____?
-No, there isn't.
-But there is a _____.
Oh, no! Thank you.
-You're welcome.

Level ONE Unit FOURTEEN
Let's play at the store!

14.3 Reading

This is my favorite store!

There are beautiful blouses here.
There are purple blouses; red blouses,
and my favorite: WHITE blouses!
There are also elegant shoes here.
There are white shoes; there are black shoes,
and my favorite: PURPLE shoes!
There are also new pants here.
There are brown pants; there are white pants,
and my favorite: PINK pants!
And there are beautiful skirts here.
There are purple skirts, there are white skirts,
and my favorite: BROWN skirts!
For sure, this is my favorite store!

Answer the questions

Are there brown shoes?
No, there aren't. But there are
_____.

Are there black blouses?
No, there aren't. But there are
_____.

Are there purple pants?
No, there aren't. But there are
_____.

Are there black skirts?
No, there aren't. But there are
_____.

What is there in my favorite store?

There are:
- ❏ purple blouses
- ❏ green blouses
- ❏ orange blouses

My favorite blouse is:
- ❏ pink blouse
- ❏ white blouse
- ❏ purple blouse

There are:
- ❏ blue shoes
- ❏ black shoes
- ❏ red shoes

Favorite shoes are:
- ❏ white shoes
- ❏ red shoes
- ❏ purple shoes

Level ONE Unit FOURTEEN
Let's play at the store!

Complete the reading with the words from the box below

This is my favorite store!
There are beautiful blouses here.
There are _____ blouses; _____ blouses, and my favorite: _____ blouses!
There are also elegant shoes here.
There are _____ shoes; there are _____ shoes, and my favorite: _____ shoes!
There are also new pants here.
There are _____ pants; there are _____ pants, and my favorite: _____ pants!
And there are beautiful skirts here.
There are _____ skirts, there are _____ skirts, and my favorite: _____ skirts!

For sure, this is my favorite store!

pink • white • black • brown • purple

Write the words. Say them aloud.

pink   blouse
white   skirt
black   shoes
brown   pants
purple

Level ONE Unit FOURTEEN
Let's play at the store!

THERE IS / THERE ARE
It means that something exists (or doesn't exist)

The questions form is:
Is there a green dress?
Are there red shoes?

There is, is used for singular
There is a green dress.
There are, is used for plurals
There are red shoes.

The negative form is:
There isn't (is not) a green dress.
There aren't (are not) red shoes

Re-order the sentences

___ ___ ___ ___ ___ .
shirt red a is there

___ ___ ___ ___ .
are there shoes black

___ ___ ___ ___ ___ .
blouse yellow isn't there a

___ ___ ___ ___ .
There pants brown aren't

___ ___ ___ ___ ___ ___ .
an orange there is skirt ?

___ ___ ___ ___ ___ .
socks green there are ?

Choose the correct word to complete the sentence

There _____ a white dress.
• is • are

There _____ white pants.
• is • are

There are _____ shirts.
• reds • red

There is a _____ skirt.
• reds • red

_____ there yellow socks?
• is • are

_____ there a yellow blouse?
• is • are

There _____ a blue shoe.
• isn't • aren't

There _____ blue jeans.
• isn't • aren't

How well did you do in this unit?
Write the CAN DO statement and assess yourself.
Write 3, 2, or 1
3 = VERY WELL
2 = WELL
1 = NOT SO WELL

I CAN...
_____
_____
_____
_____
_____
_____
_____

Level ONE Unit FIFTEEN
Let's play with prices!

15.1 Vocabulary

Describe the clothes

comfortable

jacket

nice

shorts

big

sweater

small

T-shirt

15.2 Dialogs

Level ONE Unit FIFTEEN
Let's play with prices!

Practice the dialogs

Excuse me! How much is the sweater?
-It's $ 10.00 Dlls. It's very nice!
Yes, it's very nice. Thank you.
-You're welcome.

Excuse me! How much is the T-shirt?
-It's $5.00 Dlls. It's very big!
Yes, it's very big! Thank you.
-You're welcome.

Excuse me! How much is the jacket?
-It's $20.00 Dlls. It's very comfortable!
Yes, it's very comfortable! Thank you.
-You're welcome.

Excuse me! How much are the shorts?
-They're $10.00 Dlls. They're very small.
Yes, they're very small! Thank you.
-You're welcome.

Now you!

Excuse me! How much is the _____?
It's $_____ Dlls. It's very _____!
Yes, it's very _____! Thank you.
You're welcome.

94

Level ONE Unit FIFTEEN
Let's play with prices!

At my favorite shop!

The prices at my favorite shop are very low!
The big sweater is only $18.00 and the yellow sweater is $15.00.
The small T-shirt is $3.00 and the red T-shirt $5.00.
The blue jacket is $20.00 and the comfortable jacket is $17.00.
The brown shorts are $10.00 and the nice shorts are $9.00.
Yes, the prices at my favorite shop are very low!

Answer the questions

Example:
How much is the blue jacket?
The blue jacket is $20.00 Dlls.

How much is the red T-shirt?
_____.

How much is the yellow sweater?
_____.

How much are the brown shorts?
_____.

How much is the big sweater?
_____.

How much is the small T-shirt?
_____.

What are the prices?
Match the sentences with the price

The comfortable jacket is seventeen dollars.	$10.00
The yellow sweater is fifteen dollars.	$5.00
The big sweater is eighteen dollars.	$17.00
The brown shorts are ten dollars.	$15.00
The red T-shirt is five dollars.	$18.00

15.4 Writing

Level ONE Unit FIFTEEN
Let's play with prices!

Complete the reading with the following words. You may write them in any order you wish.

At my favorite shop!

The prices at my favorite shop are very low!
The big sweater is only $ _____
and the yellow sweater is $ _____ .
The small T-shirt is $ _____
and the red T-shirt $ _____ .
The _____ _____ is $ 20.00
and the _____ _____ is $ 17.00.
The _____ _____ are $ 10.00
and the _____ _____ are $ 9.00.
Yes, the prices at my favorite shop are very low!

jacket • blue • comfortable • shorts • red • nice
t-shirt • brown • big • sweater • yellow • small
5.00 • 15.00 • 9.00 • 18.00 • 7.00 • 17.00
10.00 • 20.00

Write the words. Say them aloud.

jacket   comfortable
shorts   nice
T-shirt   big
sweater   small

Level ONE Unit FIFTEEN
Let's play with prices!

15.5 Language in use

> We use how much to ask for prices.
>
> How much is the jacket?
> How much are the shorts?
>
> The jacket (IT) is $20.00 Dlls.
> The shorts (THEY) are $10.00 Dlls

Find the words

```
R E T A E W S X I T
D S O T H W L B S Q
M E R B W O H H L G
O I I A T Y I M W P
V G C R L R Q U T R
N I O N T L E C E P
N H M U I W O H K L
S M A L L C P D C C
J E C R U T E A A D
W K R K J B L G J S
```

JACKET   SHORT   T-SHIRT
SWEATER   COMFORTABLE   NICE
BIG   SMALL   DOLLARS
HOW   MUCH

Write the correct price

Example:
The blue jacket is $20.00 Dlls.
<u>It's twenty dollars.</u>

The comfortable jacket is $17.00 Dlls.
_____.

The yellow sweater is $15.00 Dlls.
_____.

The big sweater is $18.00 Dlls.
_____.

The brown shorts are $10.00 Dlls.
_____.

The nice shorts are $9.00 Dlls.
_____.

How well did you do in this unit?
Write the CAN DO statement and assess yourself.
Write 3, 2, or 1
3 = VERY WELL
2 = WELL
1 = NOT SO WELL

I CAN...
_____
_____
_____
_____
_____
_____
_____

Level TWO Unit ONE
Let's play at school!

Learn the activities

Unscramble the words. Match them with their images.

cguntit   _____.
entisnigl   _____.
gniroolc   _____.
gpnaist   _____.
plngayi   _____.
rtngwii   _____.
sgniing   _____.

16.2 Dialogs

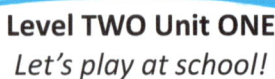

Level TWO Unit ONE
Let's play at school!

Practice the dialogs

 Is Andy playing?
-No, he isn't.
He's singing.

 Is Sandy singing?
-No, she isn't.
She's pasting.

 Is Lucy coloring?
-No, she isn't.
She's cutting.

 Is Tony pasting?
-No, he isn't.
He's writing

 Is Andy writing?
-No, he isn't.
He's singing.

 Is _____ _____?
No, he/she isn't.
He's / She's _____.

Level TWO Unit ONE
Let's play at school!

16.3 Reading

A busy day at school

It's very busy at school today.
Andy is not coloring; he's singing.
Lucy is not singing; she's cutting.
Tony is not listening; he's playing.
Sandy is not writing; she's pasting.
And Miss Patty is not playing;
she's listening to the class.
Yes, it is very busy at school today!

Choose the correct answer

Is Andy coloring?
❏ Yes, he is. ❏ No, he isn't.

Is Tony listening?
❏ Yes, he is. ❏ No, he isn't.

Is Andy singing?
❏ Yes, he is. ❏ No, he isn't.

Is Tony playing?
❏ Yes, he is. ❏ No, he isn't.

Is Lucy singing?
❏ Yes, she is. ❏ No, she isn't.

Is Sandy writing?
❏ Yes, she is. ❏ No, she isn't.

Is Lucy cutting?
❏ Yes, she is. ❏ No, she isn't.

Is Sandy pasting?
❏ Yes, she is. ❏ No, she isn't.

16.4 Writing

Level TWO Unit ONE
Let's play at school!

Complete the text with the words from the box below. You may write them in any order you wish and as many times as you wish.

At busy day at school

It's very busy at school today.
Andy is not _____; he's _____.
Lucy is not _____; she's _____.
Tony is not_____; he's _____.
Sandy is not _____; she's _____.
And Miss Patty is not _____; she's _____.
Yes, it is very busy at school today!

coloring • cutting • listening • pasting
playing • singing • writing

Write the words. Say them aloud

coloring   coloring
cutting   cutting
listening   listening
pasting   pasting
playing   playing
singing   singing
writing   writing

Level TWO Unit ONE
Let's play at school!

16.5 Language in use

> Present Progressive Tense.
> The present progressive tense expresses a current action, an action in progress.
>
> We use the verb BE as a helping verb.
>
> To make a question we put IS before the pronoun.
> Is he coloring?
>
> To make negative sentences we use IS + NOT
> He is not (isn't) playing.

Unscramble the sentences

____ ____ ____ ____
cutting   Lucy   is   ?

____ ____ ____ .
Tony   playing   is

____ ____ ____ ____
Is   pasting   Sandy   ?

____ ____ ____ .
isn't   coloring   Andy

____ ____ ____ .
reading   isn't   Tony

Answer the questions in the negative form

Is Andy coloring?
___, ___ ___ _____..

Is Lucy cutting?
___, ___ ___ _____.

Is Tony listening?
___, ___ ___ _____.

Is Sandy pasting?
___, ___ ___ _____.

Is Lucy singing?
___, ___ ___ _____.

How well did you do in this unit?
Write the CAN DO statement and assess yourself.
Write 3, 2, or 1
3 = VERY WELL
2 = WELL
1 = NOT SO WELL

I CAN...
_____
_____
_____
_____
_____
_____
_____

Level TWO Unit TWO
Let's play with food!

Learn the food

Unscramble the words. Match them with their images.

aeerlc   _____.
chcknei   _____.
uiejc   _____.
lkmi   _____.
dlsaa   _____.
wichdnsa   _____.
eat   _____.
retaw   _____.

17.2 Dialogs

Level TWO Unit TWO
Let's play with food!

Practice the dialogs

What are you drinking?
-I am drinking water.
Great!

What are you eating?
-I am eating cereal.
Great!.

What are you drinking?
-I am drinking tea.
Great!

What are you eating?
-I am eating chicken.
Great!

What are you drinking?
-I am drinking juice.
Great!

What are you eating?
-I am eating salad.
Great!

What are you drinking?
-I am drinking milk.
Great!

Now you!

What are you eating/drinking?
I am eating/drinking
_____.
Great!

At the school cafeteria

There is delicious lunch
at my school cafeteria every day.
Today I am eating a sandwich and drinking juice.
Sandy and Tony are eating salad and drinking tea.
Lucy and Andy are drinking water and eating chicken.
We are all drinking and eating delicious
lunch at the school cafeteria.

Choose true or false for each sentence

There isn't delicious lunch at my school cafeteria.
☐ True ☐ False

I am eating salad.
☐ True ☐ False

Sandy and Andy are drinking water.
☐ True ☐ False

Lucy and Andy are eating chicken.
☐ True ☐ False

We aren't drinking and eating delicious lunch at the school cafeteria.
☐ True ☐ False

Choose the correct answer

Sandy is eating:
☐ salad ☐ cereal

Tony is drinking:
☐ water ☐ tea

Lucy is eating:
☐ chicken ☐ sandwich

Andy is drinking:
☐ water ☐ milk

I am drinking:
☐ water ☐ juice

I am eating:
☐ sandwich ☐ chicken

17.4 Writing

Level TWO Unit TWO
Let's play with food!

Complete the text with the words from the box below. You may write them in any order you wish.

At the school cafeteria

There is delicious lunch at my school cafeteria every day.
Today I am eating _____ and drinking _____.
Sandy and Tony are eating _____ and drinking _____.
Lucy and Andy are drinking _____ and eating _____.
We are all drinking and eating delicious lunch at the school cafeteria.

cereal • chicken • juice • milk
salad • sandwich • tea • water

Write the words. Say them aloud.

cereal   cereal
chicken   chicken
juice   juice
milk   milk
salad   salad
sandwich   sandwich
tea   tea
water   water

Level TWO Unit TWO
Let's play with food!

17.5 Language in use

Present Progressive Tense
We use the present progressive tense to express an action that is taking place at this moment.

We form the Present Progressive tense with the verb BE + ing at the end of the principal verb.

Wh question:
What are you eating?

Unscramble the sentences

_____ _____ _____ _____?
you / are / eating / what

_____ _____ _____ _____
eating / am / I / chicken

_____ _____ _____ _____?
drinking / you / are / what

_____ _____ _____ _____?
juice / we / drinking / are

_____ _____ _____ _____
drinking / milk / are / they

Put the name of the food under the correct column

drinking	eating
_____	_____
_____	_____
_____	_____
_____	_____

How well did you do in this unit?
Write the CAN DO statement and assess yourself.
Write 3, 2, or 1
3 = VERY WELL
2 = WELL
1 = NOT SO WELL

I CAN...
_____
_____
_____
_____
_____
_____
_____

Level TWO Unit THREE
Let's play at home!

Learn the activities at home

brushing

drinking

listening

writing

singing

eating

cooking

18.2 Dialogs

Level TWO Unit THREE
Let's play at home!

Practice the dialogs

What are you doing?
-I am brushing my teeth.
Ok!

What are you doing?
-I am writing a letter!
Ok!

What are you doing?
-I am cooking!
Ok!

What are you doing?
-I am eating.
Ok!

What are you doing?
-I am listening to music.
Ok!

What are you doing?
-I am drinking water!
Ok!

What are you doing?
-I am _____.
Ok!

Level TWO Unit THREE
Let's play at home!

Busy at home

We are all busy at home today.
My father is cooking lunch and
my mother is drinking water in the yard.
My brother is eating a sandwich and
my sister is listening to music.
My grandmother is singing and
my grandfather is writing a letter.
And I am busy too. I am brushing my teeth.
It is a busy day at my home today!

Choose the correct answer

Father is:
- ☐ cooking
- ☐ listening to music
- ☐ drinking water

Mother is:
- ☐ eating
- ☐ drinking water
- ☐ cooking

Brother is :
- ☐ cooking
- ☐ drinking water
- ☐ eating

Sister is:
- ☐ listening to music
- ☐ cooking
- ☐ writing

Grandmother is:
- ☐ singing
- ☐ writing
- ☐ cooking

Grandfather is:
- ☐ drinking water
- ☐ singing
- ☐ writing

I am:
- ☐ brushing my teeth
- ☐ cooking
- ☐ singing

Level TWO Unit THREE
Let's play at home!

Complete the reading with the words from the box below

Busy at home

We are all busy at home today.
My father is _____ and my mother is _____ in the yard. My brother is _____ and my sister is _____.
My grandmother is _____ and my grandfather is _____
And I am busy too. I am _____.
It is a busy day at my home today!

brushing teeth • cooking lunch • drinking water
eating a sandwich • listening to music
singing songs • writing a letter

Write the words. Say them aloud.

brushing	brushing
cooking	cooking
drinking	drinking
eating	eating
listening	listening
singing	singing
writing	writing

Level TWO Unit THREE
Let's play at home!

What are you doing?
Match the sentence with the correct image

- I am brushing my teeth.
- I am cooking.
- I am drinking water.
- I am eating.
- I am listening to music.
- I am singing.
- I am writing.

How well did you do in this unit?
Write the CAN DO statement and assess yourself.
Write 3, 2, or 1
3 = VERY WELL
2 = WELL
1 = NOT SO WELL

I CAN...
_____
_____
_____
_____
_____
_____
_____

Level TWO Unit FOUR
Let's play at home!

19.1
Vocabulary

Learn the activities at home

Find the home activities

P	B	P	O	J	K	A	I	F	B
W	X	M	R	P	N	Y	C	E	X
A	V	P	E	L	A	Z	L	E	B
T	X	O	S	A	S	J	E	D	R
C	W	V	T	Y	P	L	A	I	U
H	N	Y	I	I	X	Q	N	N	A
I	W	B	N	N	K	Q	I	G	S
N	B	K	G	G	Z	Q	N	D	G
G	C	R	V	M	P	A	G	P	S
G	N	I	P	E	E	L	S	C	V

CLEANING

FEEDING

JUMPING

PLAYING

RESTING

SLEEPING

WATCHING

19.2 Dialogs

Level TWO Unit FOUR
Let's play at home!

Practice the dialogs

Is father feeding the dog?
-No, he isn't. He's feeding the cat.

Is mother playing the piano?
-No, she isn't. She's playing the guitar.

Is sister sleeping in the yard?
-No, she isn't.
She's sleeping in the bedroom.

Are grandma and grandpa watching videos?
-No, they aren't.
They are watching a movie.

Now you!

Is/Are _____?
No, _____.
   _____.

Level TWO Unit FOUR
Let's play at home!

A nice day at home

Today is a nice day at home.
What is my family doing? Well…
My father is feeding the cat.
My mother is playing the guitar.
My brother is resting in the TV room.
My sister is sleeping in the bedroom.
My grandma and grandpa are watching a movie.
My friends are jumping rope in the yard.
What am I doing? I am cleaning the room.
Yes, it is a nice day at home!

Circle ✓ if the sentence is true.
Circle ✗ if the sentence is false.

Mother is playing the piano.
✓   ✗
Father is feeding the cat.
✓   ✗
Brother is resting in the TV room.
✓   ✗
Sister is sleeping in the yard.
✓   ✗
Grandma and grandpa are watching videos.
✓   ✗
My friends are jumping rope on the street.
✓   ✗
I am cleaning the kitchen.
✓   ✗

Choose the correct answer

What is father doing?
❑ feeding the cat
❑ feeding the dog
What is mother doing?
❑ playing the piano
❑ playing the guitar
What is brother doing?
❑ resting in the TV room
❑ resting in the bedroom
What is sister doing?
❑ sleeping in the yard
❑ sleeping in the bedroom
What are grandma and grandpa doing?
❑ watching a movie
❑ watching videos

19.4 Writing

Level TWO Unit FOUR
Let's play at home!

Complete the text with the words from the box below. You may write them in any order you wish.

> A nice day at home
>
> Today is a nice day at home.
> What is my family doing? Well…
> My father is _____. My mother is _____.
> My brother is _____. My sister is _____.
> My grandma and grandpa are _____.
> My friends are _____.
> What am I doing? I am _____.
> Yes, it is a nice day at home!

> feeding the cat • playing the guitar • resting in the TV room • sleeping in the bedroom • cleaning the room watching a movie • jumping rope in the yard

Write the words. Say them aloud.

cleaning   cleaning
feeding   feeding
jumping   jumping
playing   playing
resting   resting
sleeping   sleeping
watching   watching

Level TWO Unit FOUR
Let's play at home!

Present Progressive Tense
We make the negative form in the Present Progressive Tense by adding NOT after the verb BE.
He is not cleaning the kitchen.
A short negative answer in the negative form is:
No, (comma) he isn´t. (period)

The question: What are you doing?
Asks an **action** as an answer.
What are you **doing**?
I am **playing** the piano

Choose the correct answer

Is father feeding the dog?
❏ No, he isn't.   ❏ No he isn't
❏ No, she isn't.

Is mother playing the piano?
❏ No she isn't   ❏ No, he isn't.
❏ No, she isn't.

Are you cleaning the kitchen?
❏ No, I'm not.   ❏ No, they aren't.
❏ No, he isn't.

Are grandma and grandpa watching videos?
❏ No, they aren't
❏ No, we aren't ❏ No, she isn't.

Are your friends jumping rope on the street?
❏ No, we aren't ❏ No, they aren't.
❏ No, I'm not.

Choose the correct verb

What _____ you doing?
❏ is   ❏ am   ❏ are

What _____ he doing?
❏ is   ❏ am   ❏ are

What _____ they doing?
❏ is   ❏ am   ❏ are

He _____ cleaning the room.
❏ am   ❏ is   ❏ are

I _____ playing the guitar.
❏ am   ❏ is   ❏ are

They _____ watching a movie.
❏ am   ❏ is   ❏ are

She _____ playing.
❏ am not   ❏ isn't   ❏ aren't

How well did you do in this unit?
Write the CAN DO statement and assess yourself.
Write 3, 2, or 1
3 = VERY WELL
2 = WELL
1 = NOT SO WELL

I CAN...
_____
_____
_____
_____
_____
_____
_____

Level TWO Unit FIVE
Let's play at home!

20.1 Vocabulary

Learn the activities at home

Unscramble the words

gniylap
_____

oomdbre
_____

slpngeei
_____

htrmbaoo
_____

aeitng
_____

ieatng
_____

20.2 Dialogs

Level TWO Unit FIVE
Let's play at home!

Practice the dialogs

Where is brother?
-He's in the living room.
What is he doing?
-He's watching his TV.

Where are you?
-I am in the yard.
What are you doing?
-I am playing.

Where is sister?
-She's in the bathroom.
What is she doing?
-She is brushing her hair.

Now you!

Where are/ is _____?
_____
What are/is _____?
_____

Level TWO Unit FIVE
Let's play at home!

20.3 Reading

My happy family

My family is happy today.
My father is eating his lunch in the kitchen.
My brother is watching TV in the living room.
My sister is brushing her hair in the bathroom.
My mother is sleeping in her bedroom.
What am I doing? I am playing in the yard.
We are a happy family!

Circle ✓ if the sentence is true.
Circle ✗ if the sentence is false.

Circle the correct word to complete the sentence

Father is eating lunch.
✓ ✗

Brother is watching TV.
✓ ✗

Sister is brushing her teeth.
✓ ✗

Mother is playing in the yard.
✓ ✗

I am sleeping in the bedroom.
✓ ✗

My father is _____.
• sleeping • watching TV
• eating

My brother is _____.
• sleeping • watching TV
• eating

My sister is _____.
• playing • sleeping
• brushing

My mother is _____.
• playing • sleeping
• brushing

I am _____.
• playing • sleeping
• brushing

20.4 Writing

Level TWO Unit FIVE
Let's play at home!

Complete the text with the words from the box below. You may write them in any order you wish.

My happy family

My family is happy today.
My father is _____ in the kitchen. My brother is _____ in the living room. My sister is _____ in the bathroom. My mother is _____ in her bedroom. What am I doing? I am _____ in the yard. We are a happy family!

sleeping • brushing hair • watching TV
eating lunch • playing

Write the words. Say them aloud

sleeping   sleeping
brushing   brushing
watching   watching
eating   eating
playing   playing

Level TWO Unit FIVE
Let's play at home!

20.5 Language in use

Possessive Adjectives
We use possessive adjectives to show ownership of something

Sandy is brushing her hair.
Tony is eating his sandwich.
Lucy and I are playing with our dog.
Grandma and grandpa are in their house.
You are cleaning your room.
I am playing my guitar.

Write the correct adjective from the box

I am playing in _____ house.
Lucy is brushing _____ hair.
Tony is eating _____ sandwich.
We are coloring in _____ books.
They are brushing _____ teeth.
You are sleeping in _____ bedroom.

my	its
your	our
his	their
her	

Circle the correct adjective

Andy is writing in ___ notebook.
• my • your • his

My friends are playing with ___ ball.
• his • her • their

Sandy is eating ___ pizza.
• her • his • my

I am resting in ___ room.
• our • your • my

We are listening to ___ teacher.
• our • your • their

You are brushing ___ hair.
• our • your • their

How well did you do in this unit?
Write the CAN DO statement and assess yourself.
Write 3, 2, or 1
3 = VERY WELL
2 = WELL
1 = NOT SO WELL

I CAN...
_____
_____
_____
_____
_____
_____
_____

Level TWO Unit SIX
Let's play on the move!

21.1 Vocabulary

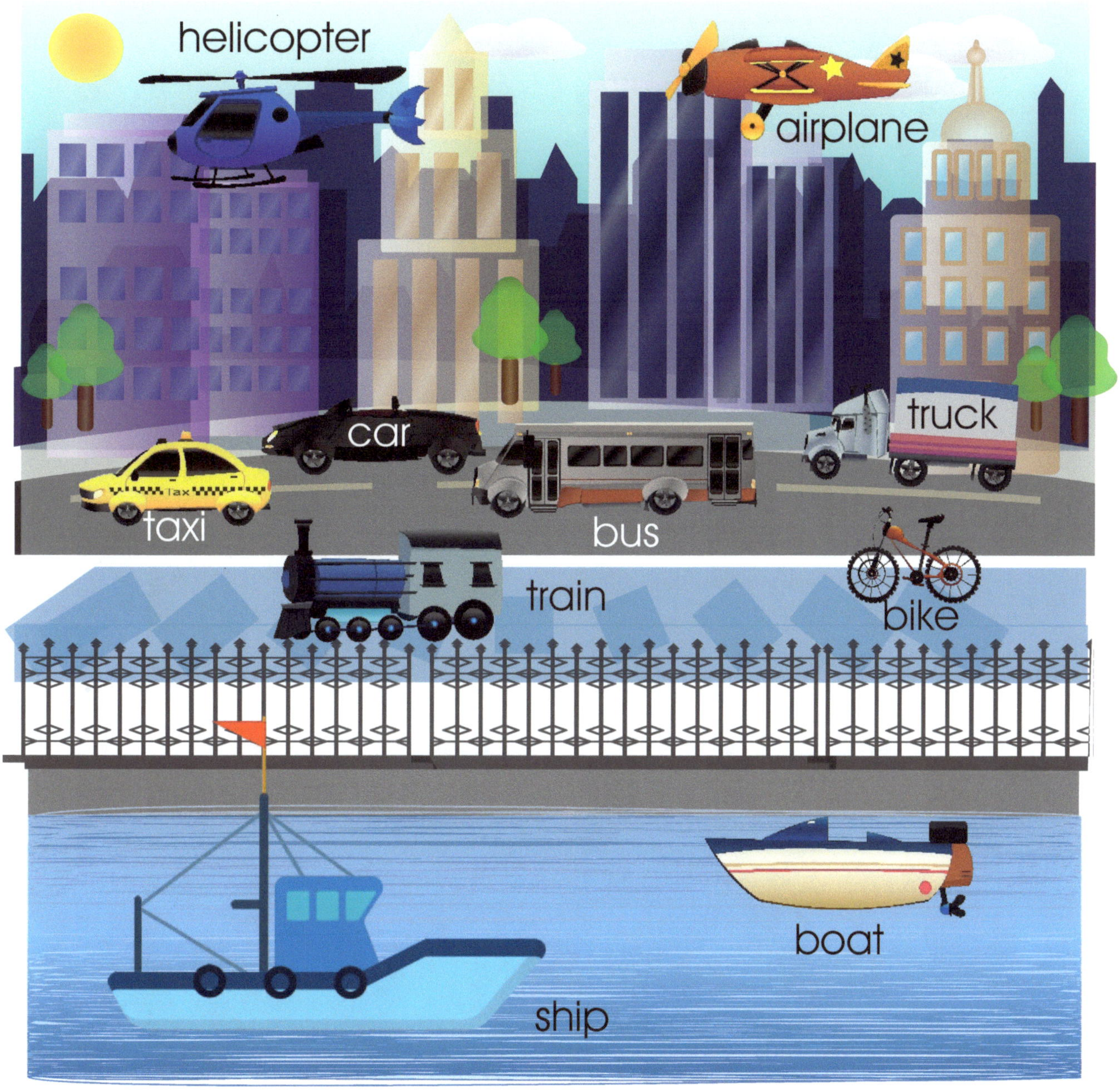

ON THE MOVE!

helicopter, airplane, car, truck, taxi, bus, train, bike, ship, boat

Unscramble the transportation word

aiaerpln _____

bcyclei _____

phsi _____

ianrt _____

aotb _____

krcut _____

129

21.2 Dialogs

Level TWO Unit SIX
Let's play on the move!

Practice the dialogs

Guess what?
I can ride a bike!
- Really?
Sure, I can!

Guess what?
My grandma can fly a helicopter!
- Really?
Sure, she can!

Guess what?
My brother can drive a car!
- Really?
Sure, he can!

Guess what?
My sister can ride a motorcycle!
- Really?
Sure, she can!

Guess what?
My mom can drive a taxi!
- Really?
Sure, she can!

Guess what?
My cousins can sail a boat!
- Really?
Sure, they can!

Guess what?
My dad can drive a bus!
- Really?
Sure, he can!

Now you!

Guess what?
My _____ can _____.
- Really?
Sure, _____ can!

Level TWO Unit SIX
Let's play on the move!

21.3 Reading

On the move!

My family is sure on the move!
My dad can drive a bus and
my mother can drive a taxi.
My brother can drive a car and
my sister can ride a motorcycle.
My uncle can fly a plane and
my aunt can drive a truck.
My cousins can sail a boat.
My grandma can fly a helicopter and
my grandpa can run a train.
And guess what? I can ride a bike.
We are all sure on the move!

Circle ✓ if the sentence is true.
Circle ✗ if the sentence is false.

My aunt can fly a plane.
✓ ✗

My brother can drive a car.
✓ ✗

My grandma can run a train.
✓ ✗

My cousins can sail a boat.
✓ ✗

My mom can ride a motorcycle.
✓ ✗

My dad can fly a helicopter.
✓ ✗

My uncle can fly a plane.
✓ ✗

I can ride a bike.
✓ ✗

Choose the correct answer

My mom can drive a:
☐ bus   ☐ taxi   ☐ car

My sister can ride a:
☐ bicycle ☐ motorcycle ☐ train

My grandma can fly a:
☐ helicopter ☐ plane ☐ balloon

My cousins can sail a:
☐ ship   ☐ boat   ☐ jet ski

I can ride:
☐ bicycle ☐ motorcycle ☐ train

131

21.4 Writing

Level TWO Unit SIX
Let's play on the move!

Complete the text with the words from the box below. You may write them in any order you wish.

On the move !

My family is sure on the move!
My dad can _____
and my mother can _____. My brother can
_____
and my sister can _____. My uncle can
_____
and my aunt can _____.
My cousins can _____.
My grandma can _____
and my grandpa can _____. And guess what?
I can _____.

We are all sure on the move!

---

fly an airplane • ride a bicycle • sail a boat •
drive a bus • drive a car • fly a helicopter
ride a motorcycle • drive a taxi • run a train • drive a truck

---

Write the words. Say them aloud.

airplane	helicopter
bicycle	motorcycle
boat	taxi
bus	train
car	truck

Level TWO Unit SIX
Let's play on the move!

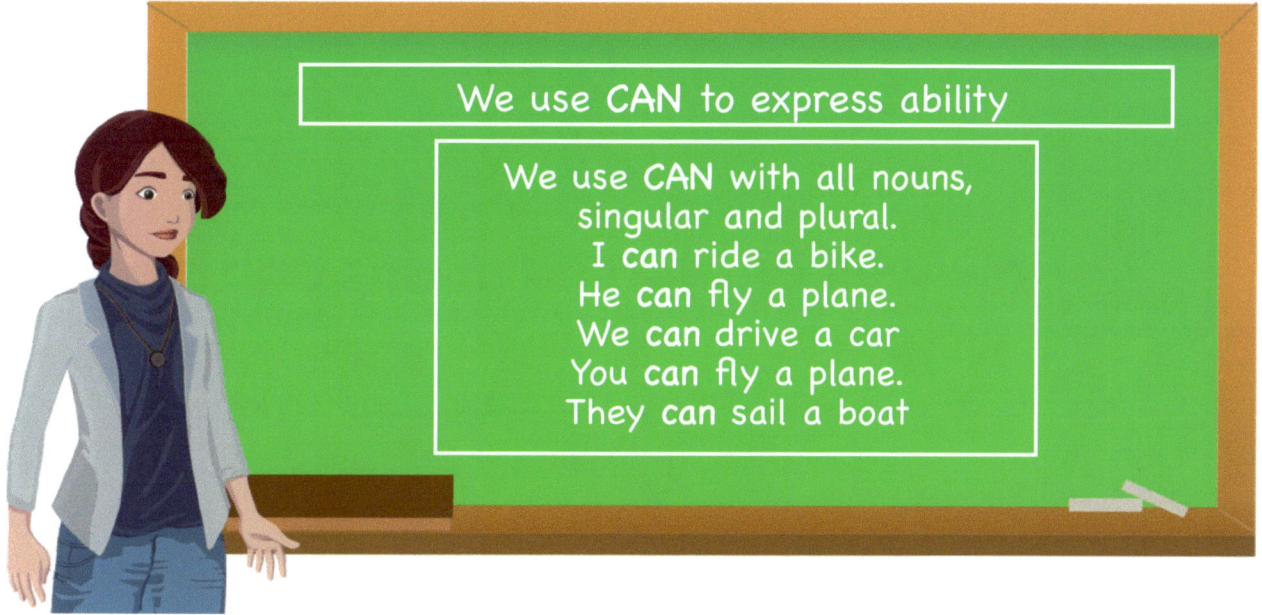

Unscramble the sentences

_____ ____ _____ ___ _____.
dad / a / bus / drive / can

_____ ____ _____ ___ _____.
fly / plane / can / a / uncle

_____ ____ _____ ___ _____.
fly / helicopter / grandma / can / a

_____ ____ _____ ___ _____.
ride / a / motorcycle / can / sister

_____ ____ _____ ___ _____.
sail / boat / a / cousins / can

Match the sentence halves to complete the sentences

My brother …	can drive a car.
My grandma …	can fly a plane.
My cousins …	can sail a boat.
My uncle …	fly a helicopter.
I can …	ride a bike.

How well did you do in this unit?
Write the CAN DO statement and assess yourself.
Write 3, 2, or 1
3 = VERY WELL
2 = WELL
1 = NOT SO WELL

I CAN...
_____
_____
_____
_____
_____
_____
_____

Level TWO Unit SEVEN
Let's play with animals!

Learn the means of animals

dolphin — swim

eagle — fly

lion — roar

horse — run

dog — bark

Find the animal words

D	D	D	O	L	P	H	I	N	F
G	O	X	N	F	S	W	I	M	W
V	G	H	B	M	H	G	U	J	L
M	P	E	A	G	L	E	S	W	I
A	T	E	R	G	E	Q	C	N	O
S	E	D	K	F	O	Q	D	D	N
P	D	R	F	H	C	L	P	G	X
L	G	O	L	R	U	N	X	Q	K
B	L	A	Y	T	H	O	R	S	E
H	I	R	M	G	B	O	C	T	W

DOLPHIN
EAGLE
LION
HORSE
DOG

22.2 Dialogs

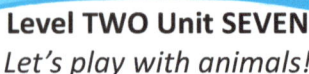
Level TWO Unit SEVEN
Let's play with animals!

Practice the dialogs

Can a dolphin swim?
-Yes, it can. But it can't fly.

Can a horse run?
-Yes, it can. But it can't fly.

Can a dog bark?
-Yes, it can. But it can't roar.

Can a lion roar?
-Yes, it can. But it can't bark.

Can an eagle fly?
-Yes, it can. But it can't swim

Now you!

Can a _____ _____?
Yes, it can.
But it can't _____

Level TWO Unit SEVEN
Let's play with animals!

Fantastic animals!

Animals are fantastic,
they can do many things!
An eagle can fly but it can't swim.
A dolphin can swim but it can't run.
A horse can run but it can't roar.
A lion can roar but it can't bark.
A dog can bark but it can't fly,
but I love dogs anyway.

Circle ✓ if the sentence is true.
Circle ✗ if the sentence is false.

A dolphin can´t run
✓   ✗

A lion can swim
✓   ✗

A dog can´t fly
✓   ✗

A eagle can bark
✓   ✗

A horse can´t run
✓   ✗

A dolphin can swim
✓   ✗

Choose the correct answer

A dolphin can:
☐ run   ☐ swim   ☐ fly

A dog can:
☐ fly   ☐ roar   ☐ bark

A eagle can:
☐ swim   ☐ roar   ☐ fly

A lion can:
☐ roar   ☐ swim   ☐ bark

A horse can:
☐ run   ☐ fly   ☐ bark

22.4 Writing

Level TWO Unit SEVEN
Let's play with animals!

Complete the text with the words from the box below. You may write them in any order you wish.

Fantastic animals

Animals are fantastic, they can do many things!
A eagle can _____ but it can´t _____.
A dolphin can _____ but it can´t _____.
A horse can _____ but it can´t _____.
A lion can _____ but it can´t _____.
A dog can _____ but it can´t _____.
But I love dogs anyway.

bark • run • roar • fly • swim

Write the words. Say them aloud.

bark   dolphin
run   eagle
roar   lion
fly   horse
swim   dog

Level TWO Unit SEVEN
Let's play with animals!

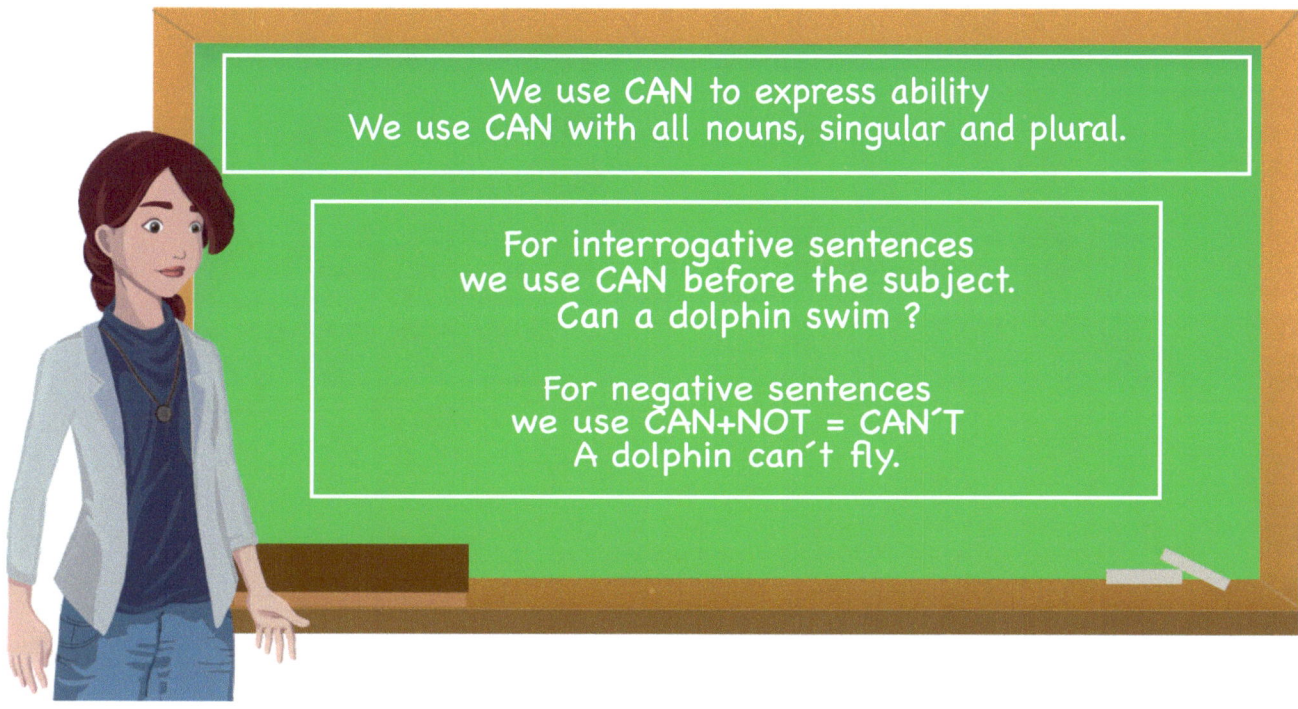

We use CAN to express ability
We use CAN with all nouns, singular and plural.

For interrogative sentences
we use CAN before the subject.
Can a dolphin swim ?

For negative sentences
we use CAN+NOT = CAN´T
A dolphin can´t fly.

Complete the sentences

A dog _____ roar.
• can   • can't

An eagle _____ fly.
• can   • can't

A horse _____ run.
• can   • can't

A dolphin ____ fly.
• can   • can't

A lion ____ bark.
• can   • can't

Unscramble the sentences

_____ ____ ___ ____ ____
run / dolphin / a / can / ?

_____ ____ ___ ____ ____
? / dog / a / can / fly

_____ ____ ___ ____ ____
an / can / ? / swim / eagle

_____ ____ ___ ____ ____
roar / ? / horse / can / a

_____ ____ ___ ____ ____
lion / a / ? / can / bark

How well did you do in this unit?
Write the CAN DO statement and assess yourself.
Write 3, 2, or 1
3 = VERY WELL
2 = WELL
1 = NOT SO WELL

I CAN...
_____
_____
_____
_____
_____
_____
_____

Level TWO Unit EIGHT
Let's play with the senses!

23.1 Vocabulary

Learn the five senses

taste   smell   see   touch   hear

My five senses

eyes

nose

hands

ears

tongue

Match the 5 senses

see *

touch *

smell *

hear *

taste *

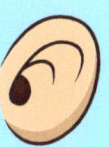

141

23.2 Dialogs

Level TWO Unit EIGHT
Let's play with the senses!

Practice the dialogs

Can you see with your ears?
-Of course not, silly!
-I can see with my eyes.
Oh, that's right!

Can you taste with your hands?
-Of course not, silly!
-I can taste with my tongue.
Oh, that's right!

Can you hear with your nose?
-Of course not, silly!
-I can hear with my ears.
Oh, that's right!

Can you smell with your eyes?
-Of course not, silly!
-I can smell with my nose.
Oh, that's right!

Can you touch with your tongue?
-Of course not, silly!
-I can touch with my hands.
Oh, that's right!

Now you!

Can you _____ with your _____?
-Of course not, silly!
-I can _____ with my _____.
Oh, that's right!

Level TWO Unit EIGHT
Let's play with the senses!

Our incredible Five Senses

There are five incredible 5 senses in our bodies.
We can do many things with our senses.
We can see with our eyes.
We can hear with our ears.
We can smell with our nose.
We can touch with our hands.
We can taste with our tongue.
Yes, our senses are incredible!

Circle ✔ if the sentence is true.
Circle ✘ if the sentence is false.

Complete the sentences

We can see with our tongue.
  ✔ True ✘ False
We can taste with our hands.
  ✔ True ✘ False
We can touch with our nose.
  ✔ True ✘ False
We can hear with our ears.
  ✔ True ✘ False
We can smell with our nose.
  ✔ True ✘ False

I can see with my
_____.
I can hear with my
_____.
I can smell with my
_____.
I can touch with my
_____.
I can taste with my
_____.

23.4 Writing

Level TWO Unit EIGHT
Let's play with the senses!

Complete the text with the words from the box below. You may write them in any order you wish.

Our incredible five senses

There are five incredible senses in our bodies.
We can do many things with our senses.
We can see with our _____ but we can't see with our _____.
We can taste with our _____ but we can't taste with our _____.
We can hear with our _____ but we can't hear with our _____.
We can touch with our _____ but we can't touch with our _____.
We can smell with our _____ but we can't smell with our _____.

Yes, our senses are incredible!

---

eyes (x2) • ears (x2) • nose (x2)
hands (x2) • tongue (x2)

Write the words. Say them aloud

ears   see

eyes   smell

hands   taste

hear   tongue

nose   touch

Level TWO Unit EIGHT
Let's play with the senses!

23.5 Language in use

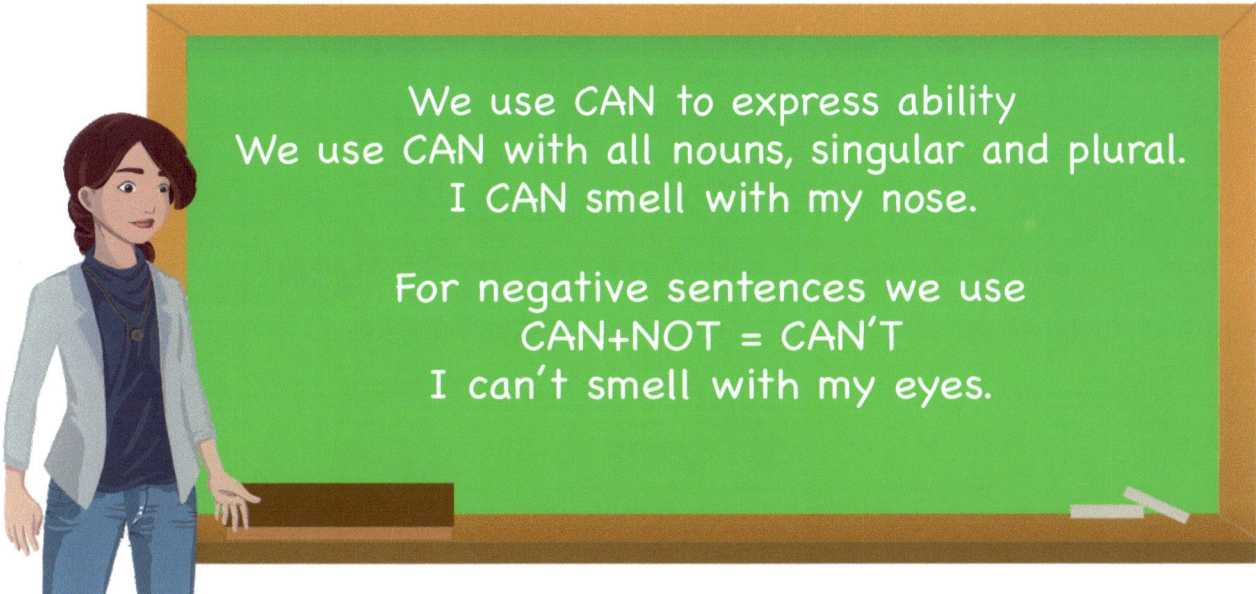

We use CAN to express ability
We use CAN with all nouns, singular and plural.
I CAN smell with my nose.

For negative sentences we use
CAN+NOT = CAN'T
I can't smell with my eyes.

Unscramble the sentences

_____ _____ _____ _____ _____.
can't my smell with I ears

_____ _____ _____ _____ _____.
ears my with hear can I

_____ _____ _____ _____ _____.
I touch my can with hands

_____ _____ _____ _____ _____.
nose with can't I see my

_____ _____ _____ _____ _____.
taste can't with eyes my I

Answer the questions

Can you see with your nose?
No, _____

Can you smell with your eyes?
No, _____

Can you touch with your ears?
No, _____

Can you hear with your tongue?
No, _____

How well did you do in this unit?
Write the CAN DO statement and assess yourself.
Write 3, 2, or 1
3 = VERY WELL
2 = WELL
1 = NOT SO WELL

I CAN...
___
___
___
___
___
___
___

Level TWO Unit NINE
Let's play every day!

24.1 Vocabulary

Learn the verbs

sleep

get up

wash

watch

drink

clean

go

feed

play

eat

24.2 Dialogs

Level TWO Unit NINE
Let's play every day!

Practice the dialogs

I wash my hands in the morning.
-Really? I wash my face in the morning.

I drink juice in the morning.
-Really? I drink milk in the morning.

I go to school with my brother.
- Really? I go to school with my sister.

I play tennis after school.
- Really? I play soccer after school.

I eat lunch in the school yard.
- Really? I eat lunch in the school cafeteria.

I feed my cat every day.
- Really? I feed my dog every day.

I clean the kitchen every afternoon.
- Really? I clean my room every afternoon.

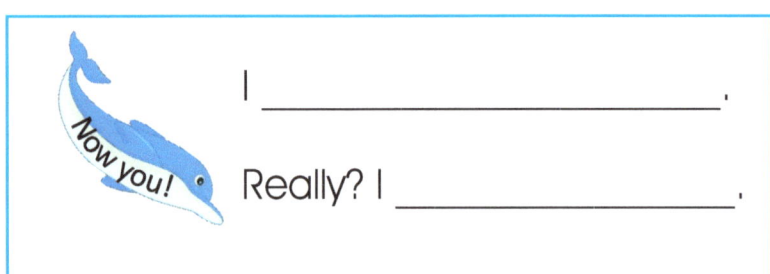

Now you!

I _____.

Really? I _____.

This is my day

I get up at 7 o'clock, and then I wash my face.
After that I drink milk and I go to school.
At school I eat lunch in the cafeteria.
After school I play soccer.
At home again, I feed the dog; of course,
I clean my room and then I watch TV.
Finally I sleep with my sister at 8 o'clock.
This is my day… every day!

Answer true or false

I get up at 7 o'clock.
❑ true ❑ false

I drink juice.
❑ true ❑ false

I wash my hands.
❑ true ❑ false

I eat lunch in the cafeteria.
❑ true ❑ false

I play soccer.
❑ true ❑ false

I feed the cat.
❑ true ❑ false

I clean the kitchen.
❑ true ❑ false

I watch TV.
❑ true ❑ false

Choose the correct answer

I get up at _____ .
❑ seven o'clock
❑ eight o'clock
❑ six o'clock

I feed the _____ .
❑ cat
❑ dog
❑ hamster

I play _____ after school.
❑ tennis
❑ basketball
❑ soccer

I sleep with my _____ .
❑ mother
❑ brother
❑ sister

24.4 Writing

Level TWO Unit NINE
Let's play every day!

Complete the text with words from the box below. Choose the one that fits you best.

This is my day

I get up at _____, and then I wash _____. After that I drink _____ and I go to school with _____. At school I eat lunch in the _____. After school I play _____. At home again, I feed the _____; of course, I clean my _____ and then I watch _____. Finally I sleep with my _____ at 8 o'clock.
This is my day… every day!

7 o'clock • 6 o'clock • cafeteria • yard • dog
cat • face • hand • milk • juice • room • kitchen
sister • brother • soccer • tennis • TV • videos

Write the words. Say them aloud.

clean   go
drink   play
eat   sleep
feed   wash
get up   watch

Level TWO Unit NINE
Let's play every day!

Present Simple Tense
We can express **habits, customs** and **routines** with the Present Simple Tense.

In the affirmative the verb has no change.
We use the verb with no change with:
I, you, we, they.
I **go** to school every day.
You **go** to school every day.
We **go** to school every day.
They **go** to school every day.

Choose the correct verb

I _____ at 7 o'clock.
▸ get up ▸ drink

You _____ my face.
▸ brush ▸ wash

We _____ milk.
▸ go ▸ drink

They _____ to school.
▸ go ▸ eat

I _____ lunch.
▸ play ▸ eat

You _____ soccer.
▸ go ▸ play

We _____ the dog.
▸ feed ▸ eat

Write the correct verb

I _____ my face.
I _____ to school.
I _____ soccer.
I _____ the dog.
I _____ my room.
I _____ with my sister.
I _____ milk.
I _____ lunch.

clean	drink	eat
feed	go	play
sleep	wash	

How well did you do in this unit?
Write the CAN DO statement and assess yourself.
Write 3, 2, or 1
3 = VERY WELL
2 = WELL
1 = NOT SO WELL

I CAN...
_____
_____
_____
_____
_____
_____
_____

Level TWO Unit TEN
Let's play with community helpers!

Learn the community helpers

doctor   farmer   police officer   firefighter   pilot   teacher

makes people better   grows food   helps people

fights fires   flies planes   teaches children

25.2 Dialogs

Level TWO Unit TEN
Let's play with community helpers!

Practice the dialogs

Look! A firefighter fights fires!
- Really? That's awesome!

Look! A farmer grows food!
- Really? That's super!

Look! A police officer helps people!
- Really? That's incredible!

Look! a teacher teaches children!
- Really? That's great!

Look! A doctor makes people feel better!
- Really? That's fantastic!

Look! A pilot flies planes!
- Really? That's cool!

Look! A _____ _____ _____!
- Really? That's cool!

Level TWO Unit TEN
Let's play with community helpers!

Awesome people!

Today we are reading about awesome people, community helpers!
We are reading that a doctor makes people feel better.
A firefighter fights fires and a police officer helps people, isn't that awesome?
A farmer grows food, like corn.
A teacher, like Miss Patty teaches children.
And a pilot flies planes, so cool!
Yes, community helpers are awesome people!

Circle ✓ if the sentence is true.
Circle ✗ if the sentence is false.

A teacher fights fires.
  ✓   ✗

A pilot flies planes.
  ✓   ✗

A police officer teaches children.
  ✓   ✗

A farmer grows food.
  ✓   ✗

A doctor makes people feel better.
  ✓   ✗

Choose the correct answer

A teacher _____ children.
 ❑ teaches ❑ fights ❑ flies

A pilot _____ planes.
 ❑ fights ❑ helps ❑ flies

A police officer _____ people.
 ❑ teaches ❑ flies ❑ helps

A farmer _____ food.
 ❑ flies ❑ grows ❑ teaches

A doctor _____ people feel better.
 ❑ makes ❑ fights ❑ teaches

25.4 Writing

Level TWO Unit TEN
Let's play with community helpers!

Complete the text with the following phrases in any order you like

Awesome people

Today we are reading about awesome people, community helpers!

We are reading that _____.

A _____ and a _____, isn't that awesome?

A _____. A _____. And a _____, so cool!

Yes, community helpers are awesome people!

---

doctor makes people better • farmer grows food
firefighter fights fires • pilot flies planes •
police officer helps people • teacher teaches children

Write the words. Say them aloud.

doctor   fight
farmer   fly
firefighter   grow
pilot   help
police officer make
teacher   teach

Level TWO Unit TEN
Let's play with community helpers!

Present Simple Tense
We can express **habits, customs** and **routines** with the Present Simple Tense.

In the third person singular we add an "S" at the end of the verb.
A police officer helps people.
We add an "S" to affirmative sentences with
HE, SHE, IT.
He help**s** people,
She fight**s** fires
It run**s** fast

Write the correct form of the verb

A doctor _____ people feel better.

A teacher _____ children.

A farmer _____ food.

A pilot _____ planes.

A police officer _____ people.

A firefighter _____ fires.

Unscramble the sentences

___ _____ _____ _____.
a / teaches / children/ teacher

___ _____ _____ _____.
firefighter/ fires/ a/ fights

___ _____ _____ _____.
a/helps/people/police/officer

___ _____ _____ _____.
grows/ food/ farmer/ a

___ _____ _____ _____.
flies / a / pilot / planes

How well did you do in this unit?
Write the CAN DO statement and assess yourself.
Write 3, 2, or 1
3 = VERY WELL
2 = WELL
1 = NOT SO WELL

I CAN...
_____
_____
_____
_____
_____
_____
_____

Level TWO Unit ELEVEN
Let's play with healthy habits!

Learn the healthy habits

brush	brush	wash	wash

toothpaste			

toothbrush	brush	soap	shampoo

Unscramble the words. Match them with their picture.

aops
_____

ooamphs
_____

eaoottthsp
_____

tthbrshoou
_____

hswa
_____

ubhrs
_____

26.2 Dialogs

Level TWO Unit ELEVEN
Let's play with healthy habits!

Practice the dialogs

Do you use soap every day?
-Yes, I do.
Why do you do that?
-Because it's a healthy habit.

Do you wash your hands every day?
-Yes, I do.
Why do you do that?
-Because it's a healthy habit

Do you use shampoo every day?
-Yes, I do.
Why do you do that?
-Because it's a healthy habit.

Do you wash your hair every day?
-Yes, I do.
Why do you do that?
-Because it's a healthy habit.

Do you use toothpaste every day?
-Yes, I do.
Why do you do that?
-Because it's a healthy habit.

Do you use a toothbrush every day?
-Yes, I do.
Why do you do that?
-Because it's a healthy habit.

Do you use a _____ every day?
-Yes, I do.
Why do you do that?
-Because it's a healthy habit.

Level TWO Unit ELEVEN
Let's play with healthy habits!

Healthy habits

Do you know what healthy habits are?
I DO!
Healthy habits are things like:
Using a toothbrush and toothpaste
to have strong teeth to chew .
Using shampoo to wash our hair
and a comb to comb it through.
Using soap to wash our hands and body too.
Why do we do that?
Because healthy habits are good for you!

Circle ✓ if the sentence is true.
Circle ✗ if the sentence is false.

Complete the sentences

We wash our hands with shampoo.

We brush our teeth with a comb.

We wash our hands with soap.

We comb our hair with a comb.

We brush our teeth with toothpaste.

We wash our hands with
_____.

We brush our teeth with
_____.

We comb our hair with
_____.

We wash our hair with
_____.

26.4 Writing

Level TWO Unit ELEVEN
Let's play with healthy habits!

Complete the text with the words and phrases from the box in any order you like.

Healthy habits

Do you know what healthy habits are?
I DO!
Healthy habits are things like:
Using _____.
Using _____.
Using _____.
Why do we do that?
Because healthy habits are good for you!

- a toothbrush and toothpaste to have strong teeth to chew
- shampoo to wash our hair and a comb to comb it through
- soap to wash our hands and body too

Write the words. Say them aloud.

soap   soap
shampoo   shampoo
toothpaste   toothpaste
toothbrush   toothbrush
wash   wash
brush   brush
comb   comb

Level TWO Unit ELEVEN
Let's play with healthy habits!

We use the auxiliary verb DO
to ask questions in the Present Simple Tense.

We use DO before the nouns:
I – YOU – WE – THEY
Do I use toothpaste every day?
Do you comb your hair every day?
Do they wash their hands every day?
Do we comb our hair every day?

Write the corresponding short answer to the following questions

Do they brush their hair every day?
_____

Do you brush your teeth every day?
_____

Do you and your sister shampoo your hair every day?
_____

Do I wash my hands every day?
_____

Yes, they do.   Yes, I do.
Yes, we do.   Yes, you do.

Unscramble the sentences

____ ____ ____ ____ ____ ____ .
?/ you/ comb/ your/ do/ hair

____ ____ ____ ____ ____ ____ .
toothbrush/ use/ you/ do/ a/ ?

____ ____ ____ ____ ____ .
Use/ you/ toothpaste/ do/ ?

____ ____ ____ ____ ____ ____ .
you/ your/ ?/ do/ hands/ wash

How well did you do in this unit?
Write the CAN DO statement and assess yourself.
Write 3, 2, or 1
3 = VERY WELL
2 = WELL
1 = NOT SO WELL

I CAN...
_____
_____
_____
_____
_____
_____
_____

Level TWO Unit TWELVE
Let's play with animals!

27.1 Vocabulary

Learn the animals and what they do

Unscramble the words. Match with the picture.

raeb
_____

ckud
_____

trieg
_____

dbir
_____

eskna
_____

27.2 Dialogs

Level TWO Unit TWELVE
Let's play with animals!

Practice the dialogs

Look at that snake!
-Does the snake slither?
Yes, it does. It slithers all day.

Look at that bird!
-Does the bird sing?
Yes, it does. It sings all the time.

Look at that tiger!
-Does the tiger run?
Yes, it does. It runs very fast.

Look at that duck!
-Does the duck fly?
Yes, it does. It flies very high.

Look at that bear!
-Does the bear climb?
Yes, it does. It climbs up trees.

Look at that _____!
-Does the _____ _____?
Yes, it does. It _____.

Level TWO Unit TWELVE
Let's play with animals!

Animal kingdom

Look at the amazing animals
and what they do all day long!
A snake slithers all day.
The bird sings all the time.
The tiger runs very fast.
The duck flies very high
and that bear climbs up trees.
They are all amazing animals
of the Animal Kingdom!

Circle ✓ if the sentence is true.
Circle ✗ if the sentence is false.

Complete the sentences

A snake slithers all day.
✓ True ✗ False

A bear sings all the time.
✓True ✗ False

A duck flies very high.
✓True ✗ False

A tiger runs very fast.
✓ True ✗ False

A bird climbs up trees.
✓True ✗ False

Does the _____ run very fast?
Yes it does.

Does the _____ sing all the time?
Yes, it does.

Does the _____ slither all day?
Yes, it does.

Does the _____ fly very high?
Yes, it does.

27.4 Writing

Level TWO Unit TWELVE
Let's play with animals!

Complete the text with the words and phrases from the box below in any order you like.

Animal kingdom

Look at the amazing animals and what they do all day long!
A _____ _____. The _____ _____.
The _____ _____. The _____ _____ and that _____ _____.
They are all amazing animals of the Animal Kingdom!

---

bird • bear • tiger • snake • duck
sings all the time • climbs up trees • runs very fast
slithers all day • flies very high

Write the words. Say them aloud.

snake   slither
bird   sing
tiger   run
duck   fly
bear   climb

168

Level TWO Unit TWELVE
Let's play with animals!

We use the auxiliary verb DO/DOES to ask questions in the Present Simple Tense.

We use DOES before the nouns:
HE – SHE – IT
Does the tiger run very fast?
Does she sing in festivals?
Does he fly kites?
We give a short affirmative answer:
Yes, (comma) he/she/it does.(period)

Unscramble the sentences

_____ _____ _____ _____ _____
slither / snake / the / does / ?

_____ _____ _____ _____ _____
does / bird / the / sing / ?

_____ _____ _____ _____ _____
? / does / duck / the / fly

_____ _____ _____ _____ _____
climb / bear / the / does / ?

_____ _____ _____ _____ _____
? / the / run / tiger / does

Write the corresponding short answer to the following questions

Does the bear climb trees?
_____

Does your sister like dogs?
_____

Does your father run very fast?
_____

Does the bird sing all day?
_____

Does Sandy swim every day?
_____

Yes, he does.
Yes, she does.
Yes, it does.

How well did you do in this unit?
Write the CAN DO statement and assess yourself.
Write 3, 2, or 1
3 = VERY WELL
2 = WELL
1 = NOT SO WELL

I CAN...
_____
_____
_____
_____
_____
_____
_____

Level TWO Unit THIRTEEN
Let's play with animals!

28.1 Vocabulary

Learn the animals and what they do

Unscramble the words. Match them with their picture.

aitbbr
_____

fwlo
_____

eeb
_____

yeomkn
_____

hsfi
_____

28.2 Dialogs

Level TWO Unit THIRTEEN
Let's play with animals!

Practice the dialogs

Do rabbits swim?
No, they don't. They hop.

Does a wolf sing?
No, it doesn't. It howls.

Do bees climb?
No, they don't. They work.

Does a monkey howl?
No, it doesn't. It climbs.

Do fish hop?
No, they don't. They swim.

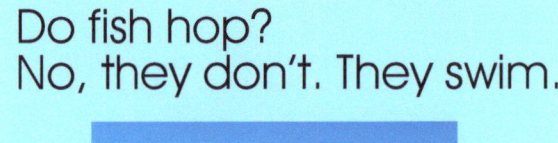

Now you!

Do _____ _____?
No, they don't. They _____.

Level TWO Unit THIRTEEN
Let's play with animals!

28.3 Reading

At the zoo!

Look at all these wonderful animals,
and the amazing things they do.
Rabbits hop but they don't swim.
A wolf howls but it doesn't sing.
Bees work but they don't climb.
A monkey climbs but it doesn't howl.
Fish swim but they don't hop.
Yes, they are wonderful animals and
the things they do are amazing!

Circle ✓ if the sentence is true.
Circle ✗ if the sentence is false.

Choose the correct negative to complete the sentence

Rabbits don't hop.
✓   ✗

Rabbits _____ swim.
❑ don't ❑ doesn't

A wolf doesn't sing.
✓   ✗

A wolf _____ sing.
❑ don't ❑ doesn't

Bees don't work.
✓   ✗

Bees _____ climb.
❑ don't ❑ doesn't

A monkey doesn't climb.
✓   ✗

A monkey _____ work.
❑ don't ❑ doesn't

Fish don't hop.
✓   ✗

Fish _____ hop.
❑ don't ❑ doesn't

28.4 Writing

Level TWO Unit THIRTEEN
Let's play with animals!

Complete the text with the following words and phrases from the box below in any order you wish.

At the zoo!

Look at all these wonderful animals, and the amazing things they do.
Rabbits _____ but they don't _____. A wolf _____ but it doesn't _____. Bees _____ but they don't _____. A monkey _____ but it doesn't _____ . Fish _____ but they don't _____.
Yes, they are wonderful animals and the things they do are amazing!

hop   (x2) • howl (x2) • work (x2) • climb (x2) swim (x2)

Write the words. Say them aloud.

bee   monkey
climb   rabbit
fish   swim
hop   wolf
howl   work

Level TWO Unit THIRTEEN
Let's play with animals!

28.5
Language in use

We use the auxiliary verb DO+NOT, DOES+NOT to make negative sentences in the Present Simple Tense.

We use DON'T with:
I – YOU -- WE – THEY
I don't swim.
You don't sing.
We don't run.
They don't climb.

We use DOESN'T with:
HE—SHE—IT
He doesn't sing.
She doesn't swim.
It doesn't hop.

Write the corresponding negative form to complete the sentences

Rabbits _____ swim.

A wolf _____ sing.

Bees _____ climb.

A monkey _____ howl.

Fish _____ hop.

don't / doesn't

Complete the answers

Do rabbits swim?
No, they _____. They _____.

Does a wolf sing?
No, it _____. It _____.

Do bees climb?
No, they _____. They _____.

Does a monkey howl?
No, it _____. It _____.

Do fish hop?
No, they _____. They _____.

175

How well did you do in this unit?
Write the CAN DO statement and assess yourself.
Write 3, 2, or 1
3 = VERY WELL
2 = WELL
1 = NOT SO WELL

I CAN...
_____
_____
_____
_____
_____
_____
_____

Level TWO Unit FOURTEEN
Let's play with the buildings in town!

29.1 Vocabulary

Learn the buildings in town

school   hospital   fire station

farm   police station   airport

Find the names of the buildings

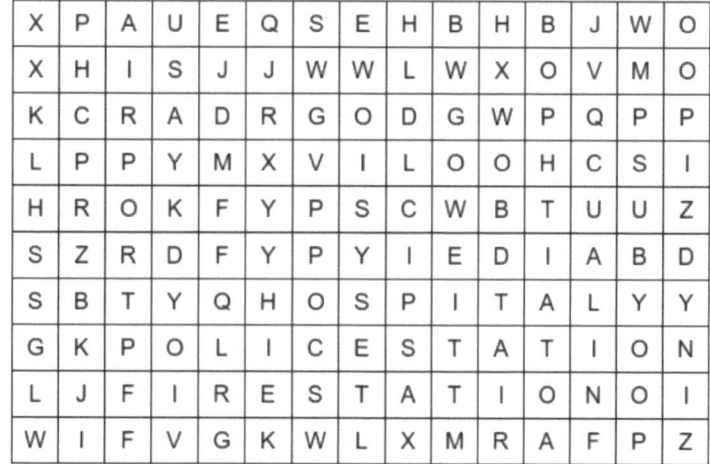

X	P	A	U	E	Q	S	E	H	B	H	B	J	W	O
X	H	I	S	J	J	W	W	L	W	X	O	V	M	O
K	C	R	A	D	R	G	O	D	G	W	P	Q	P	P
L	P	P	Y	M	X	V	I	L	O	O	H	C	S	I
H	R	O	K	F	Y	P	S	C	W	B	T	U	U	Z
S	Z	R	D	F	Y	P	Y	I	E	D	I	A	B	D
S	B	T	Y	Q	H	O	S	P	I	T	A	L	Y	Y
G	K	P	O	L	I	C	E	S	T	A	T	I	O	N
L	J	F	I	R	E	S	T	A	T	I	O	N	O	I
W	I	F	V	G	K	W	L	X	M	R	A	F	P	Z

POLICE STATION   SCHOOL
FIRE STATION   AIRPORT
HOSPITAL   FARM

29.2 Dialogs

Level TWO Unit FOURTEEN
Let's play with the buildings in town!

Practice the dialogs

Who is she?
-She's a doctor.
Where does she work?
-She works in a hospital.
What does she do?
-She makes people feel better.

Who is he?
-He's a pilot.
Where does he work?
-He works in an airport.
What does he do?
-He flies planes.

Who is she?
-She's a firefighter.
Where does she work?
-She works in a fire station.
What does she do?
-She fights fires.

Who are they?
-They are farmers.
Where do they work?
-They work in a farm.
What do they do?
-They grow food.

Who are they?
-They are teachers.
Where do they work?
-They work in a school.
What do they do?
-They teach children.

Level TWO Unit FOURTEEN
Let's play with the buildings in town!

People that help us

There are people that help us every day.
They work very hard in different places in the city.
Doctors work in hospitals and teachers work in schools.
Firefighters work in fire stations and police officers work in police stations.
Pilots work in airports and farmers work in farms.
Thank you for all the work you do!

Who works there?

Who works in a hospital?
❏ doctor ❏ teacher ❏ farmer

Who works in a school?
❏ teacher ❏ farmer ❏ doctor

Who works in a police station?
❏ pilot ❏ police officer ❏ doctor

Who works in a farm?
❏ doctor ❏ police officer ❏ farmer

Who works in a fire station?
❏ pilot ❏ teacher ❏ firefighter

Who works in an airport?
❏ pilot ❏ teacher ❏ firefighter

Where do community helpers work?

Doctors work in _____
❏ schools ❏ fire stations ❏ hospitals

Teachers work in _____
❏ schools ❏ fire stations ❏ hospitals

Firefighters work in _____
❏ schools ❏ fire stations ❏ hospitals

Police officers work in _____
❏ police stations ❏ farms ❏ airports

Farmers work in _____
❏ police stations ❏ farms ❏ airports

29.4 Writing

Level TWO Unit FOURTEEN
Let's play with the buildings in town!

Complete the text with the words and phrases from the box below in any order you like.

People that help us

There are people that help us every day. They work very hard in different places in the city.

_____ work in _____ and _____ work in _____ .
_____ work in _____ and _____ work in _____ .
_____ work in _____ and _____ work in _____ .

Thank you for all the work you do!

doctors • teachers • pilots • farmers • police officers
firefighters • hospitals • schools • airports • farms
police stations • fire stations

Write the words. Say them aloud

police station   police station
fire station   fire station
hospital   hospital
school   school
airport   airport
farm   farm

Level TWO Unit FOURTEEN
Let's play with the buildings in town!

WH questions in the Present Simple Tense

We make the Wh questions in the Present Simple:
WH word + do/does + subject + verb + complement
Where do doctors work?
What do farmers do?
Where does a teacher work?
What does a teacher do?

Answer with complete sentences

Who works in a farm?
_____

Where do teachers work?
_____

Where does a pilot work?
_____

What does a doctor do?
_____

What do police officers do?
_____

Answer the questions

Who _____ in a hospital?
❏ work   ❏ works

Where _____ a doctor work?
❏ do   ❏ does

What does a doctor _____ ?
❏ do   ❏ does

Where _____ pilots work?
❏ do   ❏ does

What do pilots _____ ?
❏ do   ❏ does

Who _____ in a school?
❏ work   ❏ works

Where _____ a teacher work ?
❏ do   ❏ does

Where _____ teachers work ?
❏ do   ❏ does

How well did you do in this unit?
Write the CAN DO statement and assess yourself.
Write 3, 2, or 1
3 = VERY WELL
2 = WELL
1 = NOT SO WELL

I CAN...
_____
_____
_____
_____
_____
_____
_____

Level TWO Unit FIFTEEN
Let's play with languages!

30.1 Vocabulary

USA
English

England
English

France
French

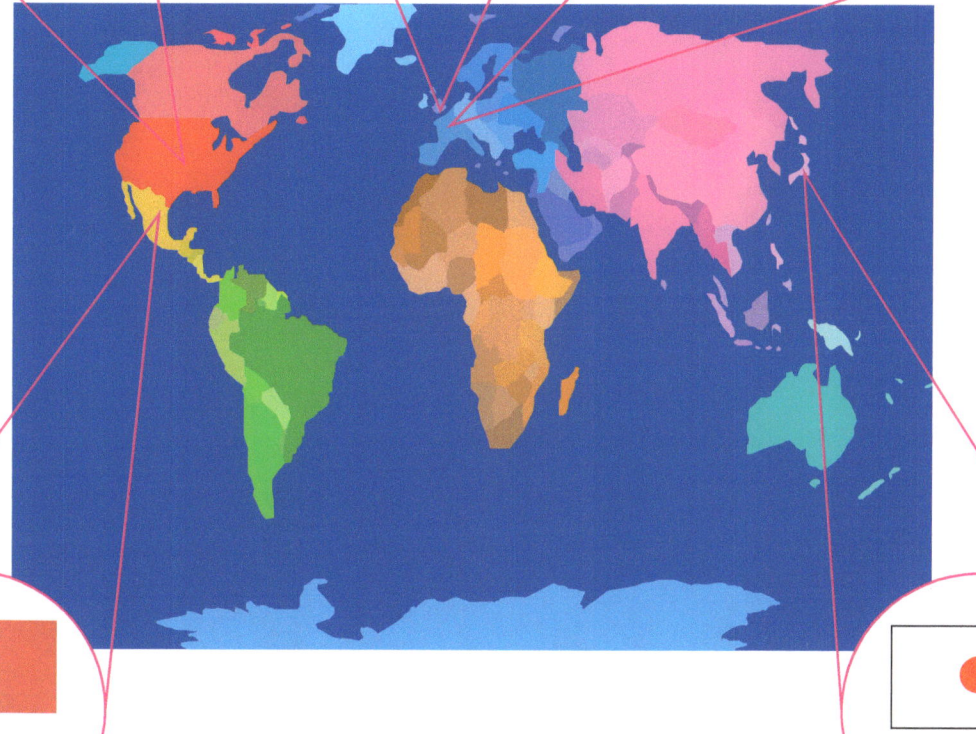

Mexico
Spanish

Japan
Japanese

30.2 Dialogs

Level TWO Unit FIFTEEN
Let's play with languages!

Practice the dialogs

Hello! My name is Harry.
I am from England.
I speak English.

Konnichiwa!
Her name is Akiko.
She is from Japan.
She speaks Japanese.

Hi! His name is Tom.
He is from the USA.
He speaks English.

Hola! Our names are Jose and Rosa.
We are from Mexico.
We speak Spanish.

Bonjour! Their names are Michelle and Antoine.
They are from France.
They speak French.

Now you!

What _____ _____ name ?
_____ _____ ___ _____ .
Where _____ _____ _____ ?

_____ ____ from _____.
What language _____
_____ speak?
____ _____ _____.

Level TWO Unit FIFTEEN
Let's play with languages!

Friends from all around the world

We are friends from all over the world and we speak different languages.
Harry is from England, he speaks English.
Tom is from the USA and he also speaks English.
Michelle and Antoine are from France, they speak French.
Akiko is from Japan, she speaks Japanese.
Jose and Rosa are from Mexico, they speak Spanish.
Where are you from? What language do you speak?

Where are they from?

Where is Akiko from?
❏ Japan ❏ Mexico ❏ USA

Where is Tom From?
❏ England ❏ USA ❏ Mexico

Where are Michelle and Antoine from?
❏ Japan ❏ Mexico ❏ France

Where are Rosa and Jose from?
❏ Mexico ❏ USA ❏ France

Where is Harry from?
❏ USA ❏ Mexico ❏ England

What language do they speak?

What language does Akiko speak?
_____

What language do Antoine and Michelle speak?
_____

What language does Harry speak?
_____

What language do Rosa and Jose speak?
_____

Spanish • English • French
Japanese

30.4 Writing

Level TWO Unit FIFTEEN
Let's play with languages!

Complete the text with the words from the box below. In any order you like.

Friends from all around the world

We are friends from all over the world and we speak different languages.
_____ is from _____, he/she speaks _____.
_____ is from _____ and he/she speaks _____.
_____ are from _____, they speak _____.
_____ is from _____, she/he speaks _____.
_____ are from _____, they speak _____.
Where are you from? What language do you speak?

English • Spanish • Japanese • English • French • Japan • France • Mexico • USA • England • Harry • Tom • Rosa and Jose • Akiko • Michelle and Antoine

Write the words. Say them aloud

USA
England
Mexico
France
Japan

English
Spanish
French
Japanese

Level TWO Unit FIFTEEN
Let's play with languages!

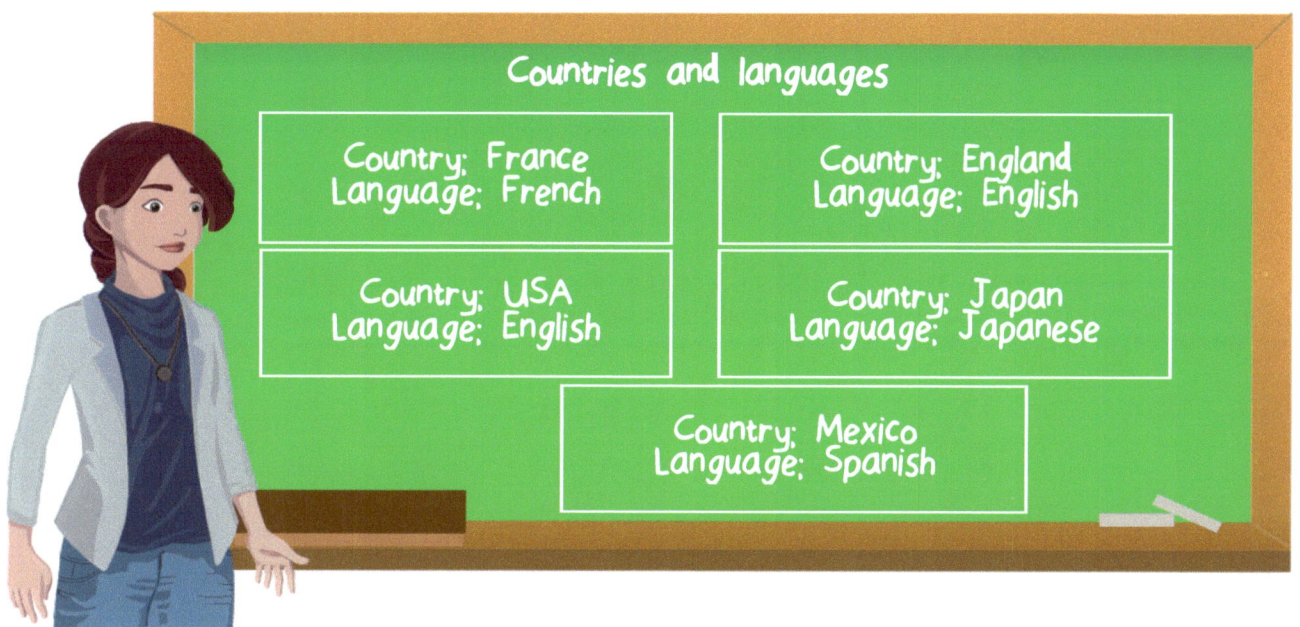

Answer the questions

What language does Akiko speak?
_____
Where is Akiko from?
_____
Where are Michelle and Antoine from?
_____
What language do they speak?
_____
Where is Harry from?
_____
What language does he speak?
_____

Find the language and country

Y	X	N	F	X	W	P	E	Z	P
B	Z	A	R	N	K	X	Q	P	M
E	F	P	E	N	G	L	I	S	H
S	F	A	N	E	C	A	B	D	S
E	M	J	C	V	T	R	F	S	I
N	E	M	H	M	T	M	R	V	N
A	X	O	M	G	R	S	A	M	A
P	I	D	N	A	L	G	N	E	P
A	C	H	I	F	A	Y	C	K	S
J	O	R	P	Y	S	T	E	W	I

ENGLAND   ENGLISH   JAPAN
MEXICO   SPANISH   USA
FRANCE   JAPANESE FRENCH

How well did you do in this unit?
Write the CAN DO statement and assess yourself.
Write 3, 2, or 1
3 = VERY WELL
2 = WELL
1 = NOT SO WELL

I CAN...
_____
_____
_____
_____
_____
_____
_____

REFERENCES

- Communicative Language Learning. Retrieved August 23, 2019 from: http://www.educationbridge-id.com/news-a-article/72-communicative-language-teaching-clt.html

- Brown, H. Douglas (1994). Principles of Language Learning and Teaching. Prentice Hall.

- Beale, Jason (2008). Is communicative language teaching a thing of the past?. TESOL article.

- Harmer, Jeremy (2007). How to teach English. Pearson Longman.

- Richards, Jack C (2002). Methodology in Language Teaching. Cambridge University Press.

- Willis, Jane (1996). A Framework for Task-Based Learning. Longman.

- Hermitt, A. (2015). Spiral Learning, a superior approach? *In Families.com.* Retrieved January 9th, 2015, from http://www.families.com/blog/spiral-learning-a-superior approach.

- Fleming, N. Baume, D. (2006) Learning Styles.

- Again: VARKing up the right tree!, Educational Developments, SEDA Ltd, Issue 7.4 Nov. 2006.

- Harmer, Jeremy. How to *Teach English*. Harlow: Longman, 1998. Krashen, Stephen D., and Terrell, Tracy D. The *Natural Approach*. Oxford: Pergamon, 1983.

- Sökmen, Anita J. "Current Trends in Teaching Second Language Vocabulary". *In Vocabulary: Description, Acquisition and Pedagogy,* edited by N. Schmitt and M. McCarthy, 237-257 England: Cambridge University Press, 1997.

- Snow, Marguerite Ann. *"Teaching English as a Second or Foreign Language".* In Content-Based and Immersion Models for Second and Foreign Language Teaching" Edited by M. Celce-Murcia. Heinle & Heinle Thomson Learning, 2001.

- Roth, Genevieve. *Teaching Very Young Children.* Richmond Handbooks for English Teachers. London: Richmond Publishing. 1998.

- freepik.com (website). This website is operated by Freepik Company, S.L., registered in the Commercial Registry of Málaga, volume 4994, sheet 217, page number MA-113059, with Tax Number B-93183366 and registered office at 13 Molina Lario St., 5th floor, 29015, Málaga, Spain ("Company"). All intellectual property rights over the Website, the Services, and/or the Freepik Content, its design, and source code, and all content included in any of them (including without limitation text, images, animations, databases, graphics, logos, trademarks, icons, buttons, pictures, videos, sound recordings, etc.) belong or are licensed to the Company.

ABOUT THE AUTHOR

Patricia Avila has been an English teacher for more than 45 years in her native Tijuana, B. C. She has a Bachelor's in Education from the National Pedagogical University (UPN).

Her experience as a teacher ranges from Kindergarten to Masters. She has functioned as coordinator of Bachelor's in ESL Teaching, as well as for various other universities; she has also worked as an Academic Consultant for different Publishing Houses for more than 15 years. Her wide experience and love for young learners has given her the opportunity to share with you SMART DOLPHIN ZONE, a series that will enhance the learning of English in a **dynamic** and **fun** way.

METHODOLOGIES:
- Vocabulary learning
- Communicative Language Learning
- Integrated Skills Approach
- Spiral Learning
- Topic Based Approach

FEATURES:
- Each book with 30 units
- Two different levels in each book
- Each unit has five lessons:

    Lesson 1: Vocabulary
    Lesson 2: Dialogs
    Lesson 3: Reading
    Lesson 4: Writing
    Lesson 5: Language in Use

- **Special features:**

    Songs, rhymes, jokes for kids, advertisements, classical stories, fables, movie reviews, short biographies, short classical stories, story fragments and weather forecasts.

Interested in purchasing a platform that is the perfect match for this book?
Email us: books@unilxeducation.com

www.ingramcontent.com/pod-product-compliance
Lightning Source LLC
Chambersburg PA
CBHW041513220426
43668CB00002B/14